MW00532090

Six in a Row

Andy Dillard

Prepared for publication by www.40DayPublishing.com

Cover design by www.40DayGraphics.com

Printed in the United States of America

Dedication

To the one who saved me, Jesus: for suffering and dying on the cross so my sins could be forgiven, and I could spend eternity with You in Your Kingdom, Heaven. You have given me the greatest life anyone has ever had.

To my wife, Tammy, and my daughters, Brittni and Holli. I feel blessed to be your husband and father. Your support has meant the world to me.

Acknowledgements

As with any large undertaking, there are many people who have had a part in making this book happen.

Thank you to:

My parents, Don and Dixie Dillard. You taught me that a dream combined with hard work is worth pursuing.

My neighbors, Pat Wheeler, Howie, Tim, and Calvin Alexander.

The golfers who came before me and who I wanted to be like: Mark Triggs, Steve Bowman, Brad Jones, Les Loggins, and Steve Thompson.

The Pros at Briarwood Country Club who believed in me, played with me, and practiced with me: Terry Brown and Jim Henderson.

My high school teammates: Brett Nelson, Mike Estes, Tommy Hathaway, John Hawk, and Byron Triggs.

Tim King, my best friend growing up. You were such an example of Christ. I'll see you in heaven!

Mike Holder—my OSU Golf Coach, Bob Tway, Willie Wood, Scott Verplank, Tracy Phillips, Kirk Maynard, Tommy Moore, EJ Pfister, Jeff Maggert, Tim Flemming—all past and present OSU players.

Ed Rice for directing me to Henderson Hills Baptist Church.

Brian and Kim Barnes, Willie Smith, Jay Lemmon, Jack Lemmon for taking us under your wings at HHBC and for being great examples of Christ.

Last, but not least, Tim Hartman, my Christian Brother, for all you have done for me. Thank you!

June 18, 1992

A bead of sweat trickled down my nose as I studied the shot. I'd made it in my head a million times. I'd lived this moment over and over and over until the dream became a reality. Silence pursued. This was my moment.

Let's back up. Day one of the U.S. Open, 1992, I, Andy Dillard—a fairly unknown golf prodigy, walked to the tee box, Weed handed me my two iron, I envisioned exactly where my Titleist would go, and sent that little piece of indented resin soaring through the air. It ended up directly in the middle of the fairway. As fate would have it, I ended up 160 yards to the pin for my second shot, which was a perfect seven iron. I faded my seven iron 15 feet below the pin. The putt was an uphill right to left putt, an easy putt for a right-handed player. I could see this putt and feel it and I stroked it; it went directly into the hole. I just birdied the first hole of the U.S. Open.

Because I was relatively unknown, I received a polite acknowledgement from those who happened to catch my first hole. I wasn't there to birdie the first hole, though; I was there to win.

Because I wasn't expected to win, I was able to play my game my way without the external pressure. My confidence had never been higher, my focus was on point, and the level of my game was, for lack of a better phrase, stupid good. You might say, I was playing the best I'd ever played.

Hole two went about the same way—every shot was perfect. The only difference was a few more people took notice. I was still in my own head— not the crowd's—and played through like I was the only guy on the course. I just birdied the second hole of the U.S. Open. Only this time, when I finished the hole, the people who had planted themselves at the second hole took up their belongings and followed me to hole 3. I was garnering attention. I never minded being the center of attention, so I had no issues. Besides, with each hole I birdied, my confidence increased in direct proportion to the size of the crowd.

Hole 3. The same. When I made the third birdie, the atmosphere changed. There was a charge, an electric current, and people were getting excited.

The first three holes. Three birdies. Had it been done before? I had no idea and, honestly, it didn't cross my mind. With each hole, as the crowd grew, their excitement caused my confidence to go up a notch. I was in the game, living the moment, and because I was so broke and focused, I didn't have time to allow my nerves to affect my game.

Hole four. This time, people started hearing about the kid, the underdog, who had just birdied his first three holes. They wanted to see history in the making and if I had taken the time to look, I would have seen people moving toward me from every direction. The fourth hole is near the middle of the golf course, and more people were around. More people were watching. Hole four was a relatively easy hole and once again I hit a two iron off the tee. I had a pitching wedge to the hole, which was an easy shot. The green was elevated, and I couldn't see where my ball ended up, but I knew by the roar of the crowd that I had hit it close. Two feet. I easily tapped it in for my fourth birdie. The crowd erupted.

I made my way to hole five. Now, a large crowd had gathered. Hole five is a tough par three. Any player in the field hopes to make par on this hole. I had 175 yards to the pin. A perfect cut five iron. As I hit the shot, I knew it was good. Once again, another elevated green, and I couldn't see where my ball stopped but the roar of the crowd told it was a great shot. My ball was about 12 to 15 feet from the hole. As I approached the green, I could see the crowd gathering and getting extremely boisterous. There are leader boards all over the course and each time I made birdie, more people took notice and wanted to see what was happening. People wanted to see who was making all these birdies. They wanted to be part of what was current and relevant. As I made the fifth birdie, the crowd went nuts. They started chanting, "Bubba, Bubba, Bubba." The decibel of the crowd was nearly deafening.

Now, we can go back to the sixth hole. Thousands lined the tee box, the fairway, and the greens. More were running toward me. My name was being shouted. Men. Women. Children. The sweat sent a chill down my spine. It didn't matter. I didn't allow my mind to go anywhere but where I wanted the ball to go. I was in the zone, and nothing could take that from me.

The weather was perfect, the crowd respectful, the world watching as my life hung in the balance.

This is it, Andy. Do you have what it takes? Are you your father's son?

I wiped the moisture from my forehead. To the average attendee, a record high day of 60 degrees at Pebble Beach would still hold a chill. Between nerves, exertion, a few extra pounds, and a clear, sunny day, I managed to work up a sweat.

I gauged the wind and replayed the advice I'd received from Scott Verplank: Andy, you've got this. You have as good or better eye to hand coordination as anyone. Just look where you want the ball to go and hit it.

My drive went straight down the fairway. My second shot went slightly into the rough. As I got to my third shot into the green, I knew it was extremely difficult. At that time, I was doing nothing more than trying to make par. My chip went 20 feet past the hole and all I was trying to do was two putt and make par to get out of there. As fate would have it, as I stroked my birdie putt, I hit it way too firm. It hit the back of the hole then dropped in.

The silence immediately turned to a thunderous wave of explosions as the crowd heard the news: Andy made six in a row! I could almost feel the earth shake from the sudden eruption of screams and laughter, joy, and excitement. It was like the crowd achieved this sixth birdie with me—and they did. I was the golden boy. I came out of apparently nowhere and topped the leader board.

As we walked to the seventh tee, Bob Estes told me that had to be some kind of record. And I asked, "What's that?" He said, "You just birdied the first six holes in the U.S. Open."

I had no idea the significance of what I had just done. I was just playing golf, wanting to get off to a good start in the tournament so I could make some extra money from Titleist. It wasn't about the glory. It was about making my truck payment.

I grinned and whispered to myself, Andy, welcome to the U.S. Open.

Part 1 – The Dream

Chapter 1

"Golf, like measles, should be caught young."
— P.G. Wodehouse

There comes a time in every successful man's life when he has to look back to see where he came from, to remember his roots and his why. I have spent hours in this chair in my third garage man cave staring at a photo of me on the leaderboard at the U.S. Open. Hours. Hours of deliberating. Hours of asking what happened, how it could have happened and why it happened. Hours of asking myself this question; how and why did I not win this golf tournament?

The photo seemed to stare back at me, haunting me, taunting me, goading me into being angry or bitter, and while I admit those were early-days reactions, those are not what I feel today. There were moments I wanted to throw the photo into the fireplace. There were also moments the photo brought me to tears. I don't know why I keep it out. Then again, yes, yes, I do.

If we forget where we have come from, what we endured to get where we are, then we're prone to make the same mistakes over and over again. On a daily basis, this photo serves as a reminder to what is important in life—what really matters. For thirteen years I found myself reliving those four days. Examining them in great detail, to only shake my head in wonder. Depression became a state of being. The only time I truly felt alive was on the golf course. I continued to play professional golf for eleven years. I retired in 2003.

Golf is great. I still love to play, to teach, and to reminisce. But golf no longer ranks as the most important aspect of my life. In fact, golf has moved quite a way down the list. You ask, what has changed? And why? Well, to answer those questions and more, I'll need to start at the beginning.

I was about ten years old, eyeing a twenty-foot putt on our local miniature golf course when the Coke delivery guy tossed out a bet. "I'll bet you a buck you can't make that putt."

I looked at him, looked at the hole, then looked back at him. My buddy reminded me I'd made that putt pretty much every time I'd attempted it. I didn't have a dime to my name, let alone a buck, but why not? I nodded. I knew I could make it, so I called the Coke man out on his bet, made the putt, then held out my hand for the payout. Later my mother asked me, "What would you have done if you hadn't of made the putt?"

I responded, "It never crossed my mind." And it hadn't. I had no doubt whatsoever I was gonna make the putt. My love affair with the game of golf had begun much earlier, but that was the day I could see how golf could benefit me financially. I may not have had the right words or a great plan, but I knew golf could give me a life I wanted.

The simple fact my mother asked me what would have happened had I not made the shot tells you volumes about my mother. Had my father been there, he would have asked the same question. My parents encouraged me every minute of every day to do or be whatever I wanted to do or be. As an only child, my parents encouraged me in everything I did.

My dad was a high school football coach, and he knew how the power of sports and sportsmanship could impact a kid's life. He and my mother did everything they could to encourage me in every area of my life. I had it good. I was blessed and I never heard the words, you can't. Perhaps that is why I was always staring out the school classroom window dreaming. I got into trouble more than once for dreaming. Boy, did I dream big.

I started out playing baseball. Believe it or not, I was a better baseball player than a golfer. The sound of that ball hitting the bat still gives me chills. I was in the sixth grade—and being the kid who would pretty much try anything—I took my bike up a ramp and met a tree face to face. You'd think I would have considered a tree as an immovable object, but I suppose, being 12, I didn't exactly think about consequences or cause and effect. I probably didn't realize the tree was even there until I was introduced at close range.

My leg hurt for days. I couldn't run. Most days I limped. We were old school. I told my dad and he said, "Tough it out. You'll be fine." We didn't know it, but I had broken my leg. My days of playing baseball were over. I could still limp through a golf game, so I continued to play.

In the seventh grade, I played football. Back then, and who knows, it's probably the same these days, for every N—needs improvement—on my report card, I had to do 100 yards of bear crawls and for every U—unsatisfactory—I had to do 200 yards of bear crawls. If you don't know what a bear crawl is, you're basically crossing the football field on your hands and feet in a bear-like crawl, thus the name, Bear Crawl.

A football field is 100 yards. I had a half dozen Ns and a half dozen Us. You do the math. Needless to say, I didn't play football for very long. Besides, I was a chubby kid and running really held no appeal. Everything pointed toward golf. Chubby kids can play golf and, as it turned out, some can play very well.

Chapter 2

"You don't know what pressure is until you play for five bucks with only two bucks in your pocket." — Lee Trevino

Being broke sucks. If you disagree with that statement, then you've never been broke. People tell me having money brings on a whole new set of problems. Well, I'd like to experience that for myself.

They also say golf is a rich man's sport. I beg to differ. Don't get me wrong, I wanted to be rich. But I wasn't that kid. I wasn't the kid from the fancy country club using his family money to practice on fancy golf courses. I didn't have a trust fund or grandparents who were living their expired dreams through me. In fact, my dad helped me get a hardship license when I was 15 so I could get back and forth to the golf course. He said, "Andy, this is your job, and you need to be able to get to work. You have a chance to get a scholarship and have your college paid for." So, while I wasn't initially working at the golf course for pay, I was definitely working. And yes, I did end up doing many different jobs around the course to earn money to pay for my practice time. Even though I was an only child, my parents did not hand me just anything I wanted. I was expected to work.

In 1970 my dad joined Briarwood Country Club, the blue-collar club, in Tyler, Texas. The dues were $25 a month and he didn't know how we'd cover them. I worked there, I played there, and I gambled there. I learned a lot at that club. My very first tournament was at the Pine Crest Golf Club in Longview, Texas, a mere 30 miles from Tyler. I remember Skeeter Irby beat me and I wasn't too happy about it. He eventually traded in his golf clubs for a basketball and played high school ball. I'm sure he could have gone far in golf had his heart been in it. How do I know? Well, he beat me, and I was pretty darn good. I thought pretty highly of myself back then. Maybe a bit too highly.

One evening I was watching the Tom Landry Show and his guest was Ed "Too Tall" Jones and he mentioned he would drive around Dallas on game day mornings listening to music to get psyched up for the football games. I thought, I should do that. So, my ritual before practice times and tournaments included driving around the loop listening to Taking Care of Business by Bachman Turner Overdrive or Snakeskin Cowboys by Ted Nugent. Picture it with me: 1968 Mustang, windows down, the Texas wind blowing, the heat scorching, and me with my arm hanging out the window while singing along. Life was pretty good. I was living the dream.

As I drove, I'd get fired up and I'd never had a problem with dreaming big. Before it was a thing, I visualized my future. I clearly saw myself at the 18th hole and my name being announced as the winner of the U.S. Open. I saw the crowds going wild, chanting my name, and screaming, "He did it! He did it!" Maybe because they were young and the new hotshots on the professional tour, but I always pictured myself winning against Fuzzy Zoeller and Greg Norman. Fuzzy is only 9 years older than me and Greg is only five years older than me. I looked up to both of them, as they were two of the greatest players on tour. I attribute that thinking to my youth since there were so many other great players out there. Years later, after I played them on the pro tour, they turned out to be two of the great legends of golf. Both were phenomenal players. I have a lot of respect and admiration for them to this day.

There were two things I caught onto really quick—almost as fast as I learned how to make a putt from 20 feet—gambling and cussing. I haven't met a great golfer yet who hasn't bet on himself playing golf. I learned early. Terry Brown was our club pro, and we would play for $25 a hole. Mike Craft would back me, we called him Crafty. He would drive around in his cart and Terry would give crafty and me the business and we would give it right back; we called it needling. Growing up at Briarwood, if you didn't needle someone, you didn't like him. That was part of the game. I had learned the game of having a sharp mouth which could bother my opponents. I've been gambling and loving it ever since. I made more money gambling with the kids and members of Briarwood than I did working at the clubhouse. Some people have asked me how I can love gambling. I ask them if they're in the stock market. Same thing, right? Both are gambling. Both are risks. One is considered a sin and one is the smart way to make money. To me, they're both a risk—both a gamble. I have more fun with the hands-on approach.

As far as the cussing goes, it was second nature. I felt like I found my people on the golf course. I fit right in. I got a butt whooping at school more than once for my potty mouth. Dad would just tell our principal, "He's been cussing since he was knee-high to a grasshopper. Just paddle him and send him back to class." I'm still working on cleaning that up. It's a process.

I was fifteen years old when I participated in my first Calcutta. There was beer, barbecue, golf, and money—four of my favorite things. The specific rules vary depending on where the Calcutta is being held and who is organizing it, but the core rules are pretty much the same across the board. All the golfers are auctioned off to the highest bidder. The contest could involve eighteen holes or as little as two. In my case, it was a two-hole contest and there were eight winners. The one who bet on the winning golfer takes the highest percentage in winnings, second place gets a little less, third even less, etc. Typically, the winners give 10% or so of the winnings to the golfer that made them some money. I came in eighth place. Technically, I was an amateur golfer and wasn't really allowed to make money—that privilege is reserved for professionals—but sometimes you gotta bend the rules a little. Besides, the sheriff was busy elsewhere with a little extra cash in his pocket. Calcutta golf is a blast, and every great player has taken part in at least one over the course of their career.

The older I got, the more I realized, while golf may not be a rich man's sport, the man must have some money to operate with. When I was a junior golfer, my parents helped me get where I needed to go and made sure I had a place to lay my head and food to eat. After receiving a full scholarship to Oklahoma State University, the college made sure I had what I needed. After college, it came down to me. I turned pro and suddenly I realized how important making money was. Isn't that how it goes? Kids rarely realize just how good they have it when mom and dad are providing their every need. Reality hits you smack in the face when you're suddenly responsible for your own success. I was no different.

I was playing less tournaments than I ever had. I really didn't have the funds for all the travel and entry fees. Golf is expensive! I was still playing, but I was sticking around home to do it. I was making enough money gambling that I couldn't afford to leave town. One day at a local course, a friend was playing with me, and he asked, "How have the tournaments been going?" I shrugged it off, not giving him a real answer. When you're broke and your friends aren't, it's kind of hard to explain. He figured it out and told me as long as he remained anonymous, he would sponsor me. I was back in the game.

Chapter 3

"The road to success is always under construction." — Arnold Palmer

Anyone who is successful will tell you there have been many people who have helped get them to where they are. Most of us know this. I certainly do. Early on, my parents were the ones who spoke into my life, encouraged me, and basically drove me to chase my dreams. I'm sure there were others—players who saw the promise in my natural ability, teachers who recognized there was something in me, family members and friends...all played a large part in my success. Next to my parents, one name stands out: Mike Holder.

I met Mike Holder when I was 17 playing in the AJGA Junior Tournament of Champions in Fort Lauderdale, Florida. This was the biggest junior tournament in the country and every college coach was there recruiting the up-and-coming talent. He was the coach for Oklahoma State University. I didn't know it at the time, but he was already a legend in the college golf scene. By his retirement in 2021, he won 25 conference championships and eight national championships, one while I was playing under him, but hey, I'm getting ahead of myself.

My junior year was spent looking at college offers. I had a plethora of them and, outside of Ivy League schools, I could go to any college I wanted to. The one college that didn't make an offer was The University of Texas. They thought I wouldn't be able to make the grades. What a joke. I reminded them of some of the football players they'd had and guaranteed them I could maintain a grade average and get a college degree. I know I was a bit of a dreamer in school, but I knew I could make the grades. One semester in high school, I actually applied myself and made great grades. Not valedictorian levels, mind you, but I knew I could hold my own. I still don't know what possessed me that year to apply myself. Grades didn't motivate me like the PGA tour did. Maybe I was just seeing if I could do it.

My plan was to attend Texas A&M. I knew some players who'd gone to Texas A&M, and I thought knowing them would make any transition from high school golf to college golf a little easier. When OSU invited me for a weekend, I went to just get away and have a good time. In fact, I had a great time. Coach was an excellent salesman and sold me on winning four national championships and playing and practicing with the best players in the country every day. The idea of a national championship really got me fired up and I told my parents on our way home I was going to OSU. My parents were 100% surprised and supportive.

I ended up going with Oklahoma State University because they had the best golf program in the country. I had a full scholarship.

Nothing could have prepared me for college life. It was unlike anything I'd ever experienced. You could say I encountered a bit of culture shock. I was six and a half hours from home. For the first time, I was away from my parents' influence. Some of the guys at Oklahoma State had had extensive golf instruction and were well ahead of me mechanically in their golf game. I'd never had a lesson in my life. I was operating on raw talent and an old set of clubs that I still have and treasure to this day.

I'd failed to make the cut for the Guadalajara Open, and what a disappointment that was. Afterward, I had mandatory daily practice. Not because of the Guadalajara tournament, but because Coach was tough and felt I needed pushing. I guess he thought I needed pushing more than most.

Since I'd failed to qualify for the tournament in Mexico, I'd been hitting the ball poorly. I went home on break and took out the first set of clubs I'd owned and started hitting the ball great, so I took them back to Stillwater with me. I had these clubs at practice and called Coach over to watch me hit a few.

Coach picked up a club and asked me where they came from. I told him and he said, "The only place you'll ever play with these clubs is Tyler, Texas."

His comment rubbed me the wrong way. He didn't even bother to see how I was hitting the ball. I had a few choice words running through my head, but I didn't say a word. I gathered up my balls and clubs, loaded the car, and took off. When I got back to the dorm, I called my mom and told her I'd had enough of that guy and couldn't take any more. I was coming home. My mom, knowing me well, told me not to make any rash decisions and wait to do anything drastic until I spoke with my dad. He was out of town, and she was going to try and reach him. She instructed me to drive around for a while, so, as any good son would do, I listened and drove around thinking about the situation for over an hour. In my mind, I had no idea what I was going to do.

I was sitting on my bed waiting when I heard the master key in the door lock. I knew it was Coach Holder.

He came in and really got down on me. He told me if I didn't like it, I could pack my bags and go back to Tyler, Texas. That was exactly what I started to do. While he stood there, I pulled out my suitcase. I owned very little—a couple pair of shorts, pants, and a few golf shirts, so I was packed within 20 minutes. As I got packed, the telephone rang. It was my dad. He asked what was going on and I told him. He asked to speak to Coach Holder, so I handed Coach the phone. All I could hear was Holder's end of the conversation. To this day, I have no idea what my dad said to him, and since my dad passed away, I'll never know. I do know this. When Coach hung up the phone he said, "Why don't you come back out to the golf course."

I agreed and headed back out. When I got there, the guys were still on the putting green, and they asked me what happened. I told them and they were impressed I stood up to Coach. For the rest of my college days, after Coach and I would get into a disagreement, and those were quite often, we'd joke and cut up about it the next day.

Mike Holder was harder on me than anyone I'd ever met, and I needed him to be. He was like a Marine drill sergeant in the golf world.

It's important to remember when I went to college, I was raw. The other kids had had lessons and people showing them the ropes. I had my natural ability and a penchant for winning cash.

In fact, when I arrived at school, Coach immediately started correcting the mechanics of my golf game. He and I went head-to-head regarding my grip. I asked, "So, if I don't change my grip, I'll never play in the PGA tour?" He responded, "If you don't change your grip, you'll run into a brick wall." So, I changed up my grip.

I learned to learn from Mike Holder. I learned to trust his expertise and experience. He was good at teaching his way, and if he and I were to get along and be successful, we would both have to bend a little. I learned to be flexible, and I realized that it would take more than pure, unadulterated talent to win big. I needed Mike Holder. I like to think he and the team at OSU needed me a little too.

Mike Holder put OSU on the map with college golf. He also helped me get All American three out of four years and put a national championship ring on my finger.

Later, I asked my dad what would have happened if I had come home. Dad looked at me and said, "You would have blown the best opportunity you'd ever had. You would have gotten a job and worked like everyone else in this world." I dodged a bullet. Not because I was afraid of work, but because I would have wasted a talent I had been given.

All in all, Mike Holder has to be one of the biggest influences of my golf game, and my time at OSU was some of the best days of my life. I've learned it's easy to give up, and many people do, right before things get really good.

Chapter 4

"Sometimes the biggest problem is in your head. You've got to believe." — Jack Nicklaus

A man has plenty of time to think when he's traveling down an open highway by himself. I'd just spent eight years playing professional golf, and when I was practicing in Palm Springs with some friends, I'd heard the U.S. Open was being held at Pebble Beach. I knew this was my shot. This was what I had been dreaming about since I was a kid.

The U.S. Open is truly open to anyone who would like to play. If you have a handicap of 1.4 or less, amateur or professional, you are eligible to enter the qualifiers. In 2021, 8,680 golfers entered local qualifiers. Five hundred, along with 245 golfers who were exempt from the local qualifiers, proceeded to one of the 11 local qualifying sites. One hundred and fifty-six of those moved on to the U.S. Open.

I had played Pebble Beach and I knew I could play it well. At Pebble Beach you have to hit the ball straight, keep the ball below the hole, and chip and putt great…then you have a chance to win. I knew I could do all of these.

Bob Tway had a place in Palm Springs, and we were able go out there and stay and play for free. It was standard for us to head out after Christmas to play for a month to get ready for the season. Landmark had a lot of courses, and we were able to play any of them.

When I was in Palm Springs, I was practicing with some friends from Oklahoma State, and Scott Verplank noticed I was having some issues. I remember to this day exactly which tee on the Citrus Course we were at when he said, "Look, you have as good or better eye to hand coordination as anybody, so just look where you want to hit it and then just hit it."

Sometimes it's the little things that help us get our thinking straight. I took what he said to heart, and I started playing a lot better.

I'll always be grateful to Scott. He's a smart guy and a great player and his advice meant the world to me.

I spent the spring on a mini tour. I was following Scott's advice and the ball was going exactly where I wanted it to go. I was playing well, but I wasn't getting much out of it—shooting 70-71s. But I knew I was moving in the right direction.

A couple of weeks before the U.S. Open Qualifier, my sponsor told me he didn't have an endless bank account. At the time, I was shooting some really low scores at Oak Tree and making a lot of money gambling, so I knew I was in a great place. This was the year I could win the U.S. Open.

I knew I was sharp, and I was playing well. I knew what 'good' was on tour. I was able to gauge my game and I knew at that time in my career, I was good enough to win on the tour.

First, I had to qualify.

The two-stage qualifying process was put in place in 1959 and still stands today. The first stage is winning the local, the second is placing well in the regional qualifier.

There are just over a hundred qualifying sites across the U.S. and Canada, and local qualifiers take place between early April and mid-May.

I played and won the local qualifying event at Oklahoma City Country Club and shot a 67. Next, I had to do well in the final qualifying stage. I chose Memphis.

The Saturday morning I was to leave for the regional qualifier, I went to the golf course before I did anything else. The golf course had always been a spiritual place for me, where I was at peace, where everything made sense. I wanted to have a little time in my own head before I got on the road. I played a few holes, and I was at the top of my game. Every drive. Every putt. I felt as though my time had come, this was the best I'd ever played.

After spending some time on the course, I went back home to clean up and pack. Yes, I leave the packing to the last minute. I'm a guy. I had five pair of slacks and six golf shirts to my name. I decided to take my tour bag, thinking I could drive a cart for the Memphis Open Qualifier and the next day, Tuesday, my caddie could drive a cart for the U.S. Open Qualifier.

The drive to Memphis from Oklahoma City is a seven-and-a-half-hour trip. I had nothing to do other than to think and listen to the radio. These days, with Bluetooth and voice recognition, you could pass the time talking on the phone. I didn't have that option.

I felt extremely confident. I was playing really well, and I knew it. As I drove, I realized even if I was playing great, there was a chance I wouldn't qualify. I had to get my head in the game. The Memphis Open had about 150 players competing for four spots and for the U.S. Open qualifier there were about 150 players competing for 14 spots. Even though I clearly remember my mother telling me I could do anything I set my mind to, I bargained with myself saying, if I make one of the qualifiers, I will be happy. Truth be told, had I not qualified for the U.S. Open, I would have been sorely disappointed.

Chapter 5

"Forget your opponents. Always play against par." — Sam Snead

During my college days, I learned what playing with really talented guys was like. I played with Scott Verplank, Tommy Moore, Bob Tway, Tracy Phillips, Phillip Walton, and Willie Wood, among others. The thing about golfers is, while we all want to win (because that's how we pay the bills), most of the time we're competing against ourselves. It's not so much a cutthroat sport as other sports. If we beat our personal best, that's great, but at the end of the day, all anyone cares about is who wins. That also leaves us room to help other players out when we can. Willie Wood did just that. He had an extra bed in his hotel room in Memphis and offered me the space. It was definitely better than sleeping in a truck or paying for a separate room.

We've already established I was broke, so I was probably looking at the truck. Playing with a crick in the neck might not have been the greatest way to qualify.

I had been eking out a living playing the pro tour, but I hadn't hit big money yet. I was also making a substantial amount from gambling. Winning the U.S. Open wasn't about making a name for myself so much as it was about setting me up financially for life and qualifying for the Masters. As someone who has lived for a few decades, I can look back at my motives for winning big and I just shake my head. We're not born with wisdom. It comes with age.

After I got settled in Memphis, the next day (Sunday), I decided to practice on the qualifier course for the U.S. Open. I could only play on one course and since my lifelong goal was to play in the Open and in the Masters, it was the obvious choice. The course was tree-lined and what I was used to and really fit my eye. After practice, I drove around the course for the Memphis Open qualifier, and I wasn't as impressed with that course. It was a goat ranch. The next day, if I was to keep my head in the game and do well in the Open qualifier, I would really need to do well in the Memphis Open qualifier.

Monday morning, I had to keep my attitude in check as I teed off. Yeah, the course could have been better, but it was what it was, and I had two big days ahead of me. If all went well, I'd be playing in the Memphis Open and win enough money to help see me through to Pebble Beach.

I shot a 69 that morning, then I had to wait around all day to see if I had qualified. Memphis came down to five guys competing for two spots. Again, what really needed to happen was me playing my personal best. A missed putt or drive by the other players was also helpful, but I really didn't wish anyone to tank. I just had to do that much better.

All five of us made par on the first hole. On the second, I managed to hit a sand wedge about five feet below the hole. The other players had made par on the second hole. If I made birdie, I was in Memphis. I was more nervous over that single putt than I was at any other time over the next two weeks.

Somehow, I made the putt. I was in the Memphis Open and I had a really good shot of making some cash for Pebble, if I qualified. Qualifying for Memphis took a lot of the pressure off me. If I happened to qualify for the U.S. Open, I had to have the funds to get out to Pebble Beach. Playing golf when you're broke isn't for the faint of heart. It takes sheer determination.

Anyone who isn't actively involved in the world of golf may not realize this, but who you have as your caddy is a direct reflection on the level of golf a player plays. The next day, in the U.S. Open qualifier, a gal named Sue caddied for me. Her boyfriend, Weed, also known as Rich Motackey, had caddied for Jeff Sluman when he won the PGA at Oak Tree. He was a high-level caddy, and any guy would have loved to have him. Another interesting fact is, professional golfers do not use carts. They walk. Sue drove my cart while I walked.

The rain the previous couple days combined with the heat made a guy feel like he was walking around in wet, heavy clothes. After 27 holes, I rounded the corner to find Willie waiting for me. "Do you want to know where you stand?"

"Yes."

"If you shoot two under on your last nine holes, you're in." He had played earlier before me, and his score looked really good to qualify. Now it was my turn. As fate would have it, I shot three under on my last nine holes and had accomplished a lifelong dream. I was in the U.S. Open.

It was dark when I arrived back at the club house. Guys were standing around. Some excited. Some weren't. I was in the former group, and it was tough to contain my excitement. I really didn't care because I had just qualified for the U.S. Open. Something I'd dreamed about my entire life was happening. Willie and I headed back to the hotel all fired up. We had both qualified.

After getting cleaned up, we were chatting and it dawned on me: I had two tournaments over the following two weeks—one in Memphis and one in Pebble Beach.

I started making arrangements for Pebble. Turned out, Stan Utley had rented a place with Willie out in Pebble, but he didn't qualify so Willie said I could take his place. I was thrilled. That was taken care of.

The rest of the week I concentrated on the Memphis Open and preparing both physically and mentally for the U.S. Open. I played really well the first two days, but I couldn't make a putt to save my life.

Looking back, if I had putted the way I normally do, I could have won the thing, or at least been in the top ten. As the days moved on, I envisioned where I wanted the ball to go, and I'd hit it right there. I'd never had that feeling before, like I couldn't mess it up as long as I kept my mind right, and just stayed in the moment. I'd never experienced that before.

I was fading the ball. The ball was going where I wanted to go. For once in my life, I felt like everything was coming together. I'd watched the U.S. Open all my life and I knew, I could feel it in my bones, that I was ready. My golf game had never been better.

Everything was meshing and I was going to the U.S. Open at the top of my game.

Chapter 6

"One of the most fascinating things about golf is how it reflects the cycle of life. No matter what you shoot—the next day you have to go back to the first tee and begin all over again and make yourself into something." – Peter Jacobsen

I ended up 61st at the Memphis Open. Fortunately, I earned $2376. Unfortunately, I wouldn't receive that check for several weeks. I had to get creative to finance my trip to Pebble Beach.

I had $1350 in my checking account. $300 of that was for the USGA chartered flight to California. Getting home was my problem. $400 went to Willie for my half the rent out in Pebble. That left me $650 to pay for all my expenses at the U.S.

Open, including food and paying my caddy, and nothing is cheap in Pebble Beach, which meant I was extremely short.

I found out from Willie that Sue, the young lady who caddied for me in Memphis, didn't have a ticket to the U.S. Open. However, her boyfriend, Weed, did have a ticket and wanted to know if I wanted him to caddy for me. I didn't know his real name until I wrote his check at the end of the tournament.

I believe I mentioned this earlier, but it deserves a second mention. There's a certain status among caddies and having a great one, especially at the level of play required for the U.S. Open, is imperative. A great caddy not only does the normal duties of a caddy, but he also knows what to say and what not to say at the right times. It's their responsibility to keep the equipment clean and to familiarize themselves with the golf course they'll be working on. They will be able to configure how far to the green from wherever the ball is and probably the most important part of caddying is providing expert advice to the golfer. A good caddy is a benefit to any golfer. A great caddy is worth his weight in gold. I struck gold with Weed.

Weed was a great caddy, and I couldn't believe my luck. Just having him at my side was already boosting my confidence. It was a status symbol of sorts in the world of golf, and everything was falling into place.

The problem I had was raising the necessary money to meet expenses. With my sponsor's funds drying up, I had to think creatively.

I had never been fond of flying. I wasn't the white knuckle, breathe-into-a-paper-bag-flyer, but I was the find-a-distraction-and-just-don't-think-about-it flyer. Distractions to me pretty much meant play some cards, talk smack with other golfers, and enjoy ourselves.

The chartered flight to Pebble Beach opened up an opportunity to have some fun with some friends.

When I boarded, I saw the seat next to Tray Tyner was open, so I took it. I had grown up with him. He had a lot of grit. We'd played Junior golf together and Tray was at the University of Houston when I was at Oklahoma State, so we played together in our college days too. He grew up in the Beaumont area but was living in Boerne near San Antonio. He was a good ole East Texas boy and liked to gamble as much as I did. Needless to say, we got along really well.

So, Tray Tyner was sitting next to me and José María Olazábal was sitting across the aisle from me reading a book. I wasn't sure about José, but directly behind us were John Daly and Payne Stewart. I knew those guys were always up for a game and what better way to pass the time than with a game of poker?

I had known John a long time and knew Payne from the Southwest Conference tournament back in Tyler, Texas. We played some practice rounds together when I was on tour. Payne liked to gamble and liked to talk smack, so we got along well. He really liked to give me a hard time, so I knew I was in for a fun flight.

Back at Oak Tree Golf Club in Oklahoma City, I had learned a new poker game, Canadian Blackjack, and knew it was the perfect game to tempt both John and Payne. I had no doubt whatsoever that both of them had a pocket full of cash. First, I had to bring Tray on board. I leaned over and asked, "You want to learn a new card game and take some cash off of John and Payne?" I knew he'd be as eager as I was for a friendly poker game. His response: "Heck yeah!"

I asked the flight attendant for a deck of cards and spent about ten minutes teaching Tray the game. After, I turned and asked John and Payne if they wanted to play a friendly game of poker.

Payne, acting in true character, said, "Bring it on, fat boy." I grinned in anticipation of getting a little heavier—with their money in my pocket!

Tray and I agreed ahead of time we'd go easy on each other and beat up on John and Payne. I rarely was the one beating up, usually I was the one getting beat up by Payne. Payne had the best golf game on the PGA Tour, and he also had a personality and looks to match his golf game. He was the absolute greatest professional golfer with the total package that I ever knew.

It worked like a charm. Payne was getting so irritated at John at one point, that when John was dishing out some more cash, he asked, "Do you even know how much money you have?"

John shook his head. "Nope, and I don't need to know."

We all had a good time and Tray and I both walked away with an extra $400-500 in our pockets. At the time, I felt rich. That feeling was short-lived, though, as I realistically looked at my expenses for the next week. I'd have to find a few more ways to get some cash flowing. While I felt like I had won the lottery, $500 wouldn't get a person too far in Monterey, California.

Chapter 7

"Always make a total effort, even when the odds are against you." — Arnold Palmer

As we drew closer to California, I handed the deck of cards back to the flight attendant and prepared for landing. I buckled my seat belt and prepared for touchdown, which meant close my eyes and breathe deep. It was Sunday evening, so Willie and I picked up our courtesy cars and headed to the house he'd rented. This place was small. I mean, about 15 feet wide by about 80 feet long and had two tiny bedrooms, a really small kitchen, a tiny living room with a television, and a bath. I wasn't complaining. I had a place to sleep at night. The weather is really mild in Pebble Beach, with the average high temperatures ranging from 60 to 71 degrees, depending on the month. You didn't need air conditioners. The best thing about the place was, it was two blocks away from the beach. I would open my bedroom window and fall asleep to the sound of waves lapping at the shore. You don't get that in Oklahoma. In that respect, the place was a five-star hotel. The two things I was hoping for—a washer and a dryer—were nowhere to be found.

At the U.S. Open, there was a service that would pick up our clothes, clean them, and bring them back pressed and ready for wear. I didn't have the extra room in my budget for that, so I had to figure out how to clean my dirty clothes on my own with no washer and dryer.

I knew I couldn't wear those clothes another day. If you've ever experienced a wet, humid, scorching day in Memphis, then you understand why. Me being about 225 pounds added to the excess sweat factor. I was drenched, my pants were muddy, and my clothes smelled like I'd pulled them out of a dumpster somewhere.

When you're broke, you get creative. I plugged the tub, dumped my shirts, underwear, and socks in the water, and added a good dose of shampoo. I hopped in and scrubbed everything, then wrung it out as best I could and hung them up to dry.

We'd had rain in Memphis, which meant my pants' cuffs were coated in mud. I used my hair dryer to dry the mud into hard chunks, then used a table knife from the house to scrape the mud off. Afterward, I used a wet cloth to wipe all the dirt away. When everything dried, I used my travel iron to get the wrinkles out. The idea of being on national television—which I had every intention of doing—or being on the t-box and someone noticing how dirty my clothes were didn't sit right with me. You do what you have to do if you have a big enough dream. I was all in.

Later, after that first day when I was interviewed by the press, I'd been pretty transparent about my clothes situation. So, on Friday morning when I went to my locker—they were in alphabetical order—I found five brand new shirts and a note from Fred Couples, who had interest in Ashworth products, that read, "These will help you out the rest of the week. Good luck."

Willie had played the tournament before, so he showed me the ropes as far as getting registered went. I pulled out my checkbook and wrote a smoking hot check for $1500. Depending on how old you are, you may remember when checks could take a week or even longer to clear your account. If you have no idea what I'm talking about, you need to watch the movie Catch Me if You Can with Leonardo DiCaprio. Is the movie a bit exaggerated? Yes. But is it completely out of context? Heck no. I knew the tournament would hold my check until after Sunday and then it would take a good week or so to clear. I also knew that if I finished 36 holes, I'd get a check for a grand. I was bound and determined I would play no matter what happened to me. Bust a leg, I'd use crutches. Smash my finger, I'd play through the pain. Get the flu, I'd have Weed hold the puke bucket. It didn't matter, I had to play at least the first 36 holes. I had to cover that check. Whatever you do, don't try that today. You'll end up in a lot of trouble. I'm fairly certain these days banks can sense when you put a pen to a check and the money is out of your account before you're able to configure a plan to rob Peter to pay Paul. And if you've never heard that expression, just look it up.

Speaking of national television coverage, when the tee times came out, I noticed I was two groups behind Payne Stewart, the defending champion from last year's Open. I pointed this out to Willie and we both agreed I had a good chance of getting some television coverage if I got off to a good start. When the tournament arranges the pairings, they make sure the golfers who are drawing the crowds get to tee off when the telecast is scheduled. Those are the golfers people are tuning in to watch. Everyone wanted to see Payne play. No one was there to see Andy Dillard, so the cameras wouldn't be following me around. But being grouped that close to Payne meant I could possibly see some coverage if I could get off to a decent start and play well. Why is that important? When I was in a practice round, I was playing with Billy Ray Brown, and he told me how much he had made when he made it on television in his previous U.S. Open tournament with his Titleist gear. When you're wearing a Titleist hat, using Titleist clubs, and carrying a Titleist bag, like I was, it meant my sponsoring company would pay me $300 for every second I was on television. When I heard that, I made it my goal to get at least a few minutes of airtime. I really needed the cash.

Chapter 8

"Golf is a matter of confidence. If you think you cannot do it, there's no chance you will."
— Henry Cotton

Have you ever looked back at your life and thought, Man, was I cocky! Then again, if a man doesn't believe in himself, you're in the wrong business.

There are positives and negatives about California, but that is true of any place. Pebble Beach Golf Course was a positive. Any time I had played that course, I had always played well. It was a straightforward course, no surprises, so I knew if my putting was at the level it usually was, I had a chance of winning. I'd never felt better about my game.

Monday morning, after Willie walked me through the registration process, we put our names down on the tee time sheet for a few practice rounds. Others could join us, and we had several friends who added their names to our tee times.

The tournament had turned a polo field into a driving range for the tournament. I mainly worked on my putting all week because if that got to my usual standards, I knew I would have a special week. When I was in Memphis, I knew I wasn't putting as good as I was used to.

I'd not been happy with my short game. I knew the short game was the best part of my game, so I spent nearly all my time chipping and putting. I got a good feel for the speed of the greens, working on my stroke, that sort of thing. Back to my roots. It paid off too because, suddenly, my putting stroke was where it should be. My putting was matching my ball striking, which is very unusual for golfers. You're usually excelling in one or the other, but not both. Again, everything was coming together in the biggest tournament of my life.

I credit my putting stoke to hanging out on the putting green as a kid for hours as I wasn't allowed to play until after 2 pm on the weekends. I spent most of my time practicing putting.

Monday afternoon, after I finished up my first practice round, Willie and I headed to the practice tee to hit a few balls and Artie, a guy with Cobra, and I were chatting. I told him I was having a hard time getting my ball out of the rough because it was so high. He handed me his seven wood with rails on it and told me to try that. It worked. I managed to find a club that would help me get the ball out of the rough. The only problem was, there's a 14-club limit so I'd have to get rid of a club. I removed the eight iron. I could either hit a real soft cut seven or hard nine to fill in the gap.

Tammy, then my girlfriend and now my wife, called and wanted to come out to Pebble. I had $650 to my name. The ticket cost $660. She had never been to a big golf tournament, so I said, "Why not." Besides, it would be really nice to have her by my side.

I'd never experienced the excitement of the Open in person. I'd only watched it from the comfort of my living room on television so it would be fun to share the energy of the event with someone I knew.

I picked Tammy up from the airport in the courtesy car the tournament provided for me. You should have seen the faces of the people around as she climbed in. A brand-new Cadillac with U.S. Open, 1992 plastered to the doors was bound to attract attention because only the players in this tournament drove this car. It was a small taste of what I'd been after my whole life, and I loved it.

This is the tournament I'd always dreamed of winning.

We crashed at the house that night, then Wednesday morning, we headed to the golf course. I told her this was a tournament unlike any other she'd ever been to before. Watching a tournament on television doesn't allow a person to take in the atmosphere. Something is going on everywhere you look, kind of like a circus act and multiple rings with performers.

I had an idea of what the Open would feel like, what it would be like to experience it. Tammy had never imagined it because it wasn't her dream. It was mine. When she witnessed the scene on Wednesday, she started to understand my passion and the enormity of playing in the U.S. Open.

I had fun watching her experience the U.S. Open atmosphere. We were invited to a barbecue after practice, and we agreed to go. The way the area was set up, there weren't too many places to go to get something to eat, so some burgers on the grill sounded good.

We got there and, man, this place was phenomenal. There was a guy who handled flights, places to stay, etc. He worked for the PGA Tour, and he knew the guy who owns Lender Bagels, so he and another caddy were staying at this guy's 13-million-dollar house. We were hanging out but there was no food. It was getting late, so I said to Willie and Tammie, "Hey, let's get out of here, get something to eat, and go back to the house and get some rest." The tournament started the next morning and I wanted to be my best.

The next morning we were at the course and Bambi, Willie's caddy, asked us if we'd heard the news. We hadn't. Apparently, someone finally showed up with burger meat and the stuff for burgers at the Lender house. Afterward, one of the caddies put the hot coals in the garbage right next to the garage. The garage caught fire and the whole place would have gone up in flames had the fire department not acted so quickly.

And that is the life of a golfer. You never know what is going to happen next.

Chapter 9

"Nobody wins the Open. It wins you."
— Cary Middlecoff, on the U.S. Open

My first practice round was unlike anything I'd ever experienced. The USGA purposely grooms and manages the course to make playing difficult. I get it. We're the best of the best and they want to see what we're made of and how we handle the challenges.

I had no idea—besides Willie and me—who might join us in our practice rounds. Anyone could have, including Payne Stewart, Fred Couples, or even Jack Nicklaus. Nothing would have surprised me. I was already in awe of the whole experience and having anyone who I admired practice with me would have only added to the excitement of the moment.

This was a practice round, and the crowds were everywhere. Simply unbelievable. I was experiencing a state of euphoria. This was everything I'd dreamed about.

To put the crowds in perspective, there can be anywhere from 50,000 to 60,000—some years even more—spectators on any given day in the U.S. Open. The largest NFL stadium in the U.S. is the AT&T in Arlington, Texas, and it seats 80,000 people. Now picture tens of thousands of people around the greens, cheering, and just being, well, people. A person couldn't help being excited. It was catching.

When I stepped onto the first green, I could feel the steel spikes on my shoes sink into the nearly dead green and I could hear the crunch of the grass breaking. Everything was brown, dingy. Willie told me they purposefully kill the greens and only water it enough to give them the firmness the USGA wants for the tournament. I took my putter and scraped the top of the grass on the green and I could see the thatch. It was obvious the greens were going to be extremely hard and fast.

The rough on a normal course, according to the USGA, should be approximately two to two- and three-quarter inches high. The rough for the U.S. Open will be between five and six inches. That is a big difference. The U.S. Open has been dubbed "Golf's Toughest Test" and those in charge of the course make an under-par score next to impossible. In fact, there have been many winners who have won with a score over par because of how difficult the course is. Johnny Miller of NBC described the greens as "like trying to hit a ball on top of a VW Beetle."

The last time I had played the Pebble Beach Course was in winter at the AT&T Pro Am. The AT&T Pro Am used be called The Crosby and was started back in 1937 by Bing Crosby. After Crosby's death in 1977, his family ran the tournament for another eight years. In 1986, the tournament became the AT&T Pro Am. Other than the terrain, the Crosby was nothing like the U.S. Open. Then, the greens were in top notch condition, and we played one of the nicest courses in the country. Of course, Pebble Beach is still considered one of the best, if not the best, course in North America. And while Bing isn't there and the clambake no longer takes place, you still might see a few familiar faces in the lineup of golfers.

The U.S. Open, while exciting, had a serious feeling to it. I had game-planned and came up with a formula for the U.S. Open. Every six pars in the U.S. Open equals a birdie, no three putts, and nothing worse than a bogey. As fate would have it, I never did have a three putt, and I never had worse than a bogey for the entire week at Pebble. This was my game plan for winning the U.S. Open.

I had been off the tour for about four years at the time of the '92 Open, so I'd been scrounging by, barely making truck payments and wondering where my next dollar was coming from. It was a tough time financially, which seemed to be the story of my life.

One of the positives of being broke was that I felt less pressure on the course. I was dealing with GMAC calling and wanting a payment, or how I was going to cover the $1500 check I had written. My mind obviously wasn't fully on the U.S. Open and how I was going to play, but it was on how I was going to make some money. The reality of being broke trumped the excitement of playing in the U.S. Open. It took some of the stress off me, which I was thankful for. Between the financial stress and the fact I wasn't a household name, I didn't have to worry about PR or anything like that, which helped.

The first practice round we played with David Love and Brad Faxon, two really great golfers. It's hard not to compare yourself to other golfers, especially when you're playing as well as or even better than they are. I was hitting driver, which most golfers weren't doing, on holes 15 and 16. There's a tall pine on the left side of the fairway on hole 15. I was clearing it when no one else was even thinking about it. That's how good I was hitting the ball and why most of my practice time was spent on the putting green.

When we finished the practice round on Monday, one of my biggest takeaways was to keep the ball on the fairway. The rough was beyond any rough I'd ever experienced. In fact, it was brutal. If I didn't keep my ball in the fairway, I was gonna shoot a hundred.

I was driving the ball exactly where I wanted it to go every single time, and this gave me an idea of how I was going to play in the tournament. The practice green became my place to hang out. If my putting matched my ball striking, I could win the U.S. Open.

Andy Dillard 1996 PGA Tour

Part 2 – The U.S. Open

Chapter 10

"You know, the Oscar I was awarded for The Untouchables is a wonderful thing, but I can honestly say that I'd rather have won the U.S. Open Golf Tournament."
— Sean Connery

Thursday morning when I walked onto the green, in that moment everything I had sacrificed, every heartache I'd experienced, and all hard times I'd been through was worth it. I was playing in the U.S. Open and it was all I'd dreamed it would be.

I was strangely calm. The night before I'd slept well. I'd had enough experience on the PGA Tour to know what to expect, so the only thing I really worried about was my finances. I was used to scrambling in that area of my life so that wasn't anything new. I knew how to shelve my concern when I needed to focus on something else, and at that moment in time, every bit of energy I had went to the Open. Rightly so.

The first U.S. Open was played in 1895 with eleven players competing for the first prize of $150. In more recent years, the first prize is well over a million dollars. That check would take care of all my money issues and then some. I had three goals. To finish 36 holes, to win the U.S. Open, and to get in the Masters. I'd celebrate the win after the check was safely in my account and my truck payment was made.

I'd seen the U.S. Open on television for years, but nothing prepared me for the crazy big crowds. We had a relatively easy time of parking as the USGA had special areas for us, but spectators had to park and then be bussed in. People were everywhere. We had players' badges that got us anywhere we needed to go.

I met my caddy, Weed, at the practice tee about an hour before my tee time. I had the same warm-up routine since I was in college. I always started out with a pitching wedge, then a seven iron, then a five iron, then to my driver. I always hit balls before I putted.

Willie was a few groups ahead of me. In the U.S. Open, everybody starts at the first tee. My tee time was finally here. I am 100 percent convinced the only reason I wasn't nervous was because of how broke I was. My initial goal was to finish the first 36 holes to cover the hot check I wrote. When your goals revolve around making ends meet, sometimes it's easier to focus on one small goal at a time. It takes your mind off the big picture.

I knew exactly what to do on the first hole. I took out my 2 iron and hit that stock fade I had going. I could have hit the driver but didn't see the benefit. I was not nervous one bit.

I got down to my tee shot and my goal all week was to stay below the hole. If you hit it above the hole, you are hoping to 2 putt. So, I hit a little fade 7-iron in there about 15 feet below the hole. It was basically an uphill putt that breaks about 2 inches from right to left—a perfect putt for a right-handed golfer. I poured it right in there. We had a few people following us because there are people everywhere. My caddie, Weed, said "Good putt, good start."

I just birdied the first hole of the U.S. Open.

The second hole was a short par 5 that even I could reach in two shots. I was carrying a weak 3-wood, about a 3 ½ wood, that I knew I could use to reach the green after a good drive. My tee shot was in the fairway and the pin was back right.

I hit the 3-wood just short of the green on the left side—perfect position about 60 feet from the hole.

I had an easy bump and run chip shot, so I took out my pitching wedge, which I used for bump and run chips. I hit it up there, catching the left edge of the cup and going by two feet for an easy birdie. It could have gone in for an eagle.

So far, everything was perfect. I made my short putt for a very easy birdie and all of a sudden, I was two under at the U.S. Open.

The third hole at Pebble is a little 90-degree dogleg left trees on the left-hand side. The hole did not fit my ball flight, but it didn't matter because I knew exactly where the ball was going. I took out my driver and started it out over the trees on the left and it cut back perfectly in the middle of the fairway. So now I am into three and have not missed a shot. We got to the ball and the yardage was 138 yards. It was a tough pin placement because it was on the front left of the green, making it hard to stop and hard for my fade. But I was not fazed. The thought of short siding myself never entered my mind.

I took out my 9 iron and hit a fade and the ball landed 8 feet short of the hole, then went over the hole between the pin and the cup and stopped 8 feet behind the hole. So, I still hadn't missed a shot. The chip shot on 2 could have gone in as could have the second shot on three. I took my putter out and stroked it right into the hole.

I had now birdied the first 3 holes and people were starting to notice. I had no idea how Bob Estes or Tom Jenkins were playing, but I had a red 3 by my name.

The fourth hole was an easy hole—a straight away par 4. For me, it was a 2-iron to get it into play and then have about 115 yards to go to the hole. I hit the 2-iron perfectly and sure enough, I had 115 to a back pin. In the U.S. Open, you never want to go over a green, especially at Pebble. "So," Weed asked, "what do you think?" I returned the question: "What do you mean what do I think?" He said, "You want to be sure to leave it below the hole." I replied, "I will show you short of the hole."

By now, there were people following us from fairway to fairway and watching as I hit this little three quarters pitching wedge right at the hole and it looked perfect. The ball landed up there and the people started going crazy. Weed commented, "That looks close." And I said, "Yeah, I think it is."

We got up there, and it was about 3 feet below the hole and straight up the hill. I made that putt and all of a sudden, I had played four holes and every shot had gone where I looked and thought about it going. Now I was really not thinking of anything—I was in something like a fog because I was looking at where I wanted the ball to go, and it was going right there.

I never thought about being four under, just that the ball was going where I was looking, and it was almost like someone else was swinging the club for me. Never once did I think this is the U.S. Open or being four under after four. God had a hold of the club—I was there and someone else was doing the work.

I walked onto the fifth tee and people were everywhere. The fifth was back into the middle of the course and was accessible from everywhere. At this point, you could hear the buzz and some people were yelling and screaming. The atmosphere was charged, and people were coming from everywhere.

The fifth hole was an uphill, 180-yard, par 3. It was so uphill that I could not see the surface of the green. We got our yardage and, for me, it required a 5 iron—right in my wheelhouse. I hit it about 10 feet from the hole and the crowd went crazy. I had a simple right to left putt that was a little quick, but I made it, right in the middle, never a doubt. It's like I said, "Hey, ball, this is where you are going", and it went right there. It was uncanny.

Weed is a seasoned caddie, so he stayed cool and collected. Later, he told me how much he enjoyed the experience. He has caddied for many great players through the years, but he said caddying for me at the U.S. Open was his favorite. That meant a lot to me.

He said this was the best. I felt honored to have a caddy like Weed—Rich Motackey—at my side at such an important time in my life. He has caddied for winners in majors.

When we got to the 6 tee there was a massive crowd. There were people all around the tee box and up the fairway. There were more people watching me than ever before in my life. It was Thursday afternoon at the U.S. Open.

I knew the sixth hole was a reachable par 5, so I said, "What the heck" and just hit a perfect drive with a little cut down the middle. We walked down there, and I got my yardage and prepare to hit my second shot.

Before we could hit our second shots, we had a little bit of time as we waited on the group ahead of us. I remembered Billy Ray Brown saying he had seen sharks in the water off the sixth fairway the day before and since we were having to wait, I walked over to see if I could see any sharks. Just killing a little time and the USGA official who was with us—each group has one following their group—walked over and said, "HEY, what are you doing?"

That surprised me a little, but I responded, "Billy Ray Brown said he saw some sharks over here, so I am taking a look."

That USGA official said, "Hey son, you're in the U.S. Open and you are five under par through five holes. You need to get back over there and pay attention to what you are doing."

WOW!

He was an older guy, so I said "yes, sir" (my mama would have been proud). But I was arrogant back then and was thinking, Who are you to come over here and tell me how to play in a golf tournament? You are an official and I am a player. But really, I got a kick out of it, and it was just a part of the plan. I was still very relaxed, and I got to see a couple of sharks. It was so cool.

I hit a good second shot, even though it got just into the rough because the 3-wood went straight instead of fading. It was only three feet into the rough, but it was in very thick grass. I hit my third shot too firm and it went about 20 feet past the hole.

The green was elevated so we had a great view. People were just everywhere. I thought, Just cozy this downhill putt down there close to the hole, get your par, and you are five under through six holes and everything will be fine. But just as soon as I hit the putt, only 3 inches off the putter face, I knew I had hit it too hard. It went off like a bomb.

The putt was red hot, like it was shot out of a cannon, and I knew it would go at least 15 feet past the hole. But somehow, it hit the hole and went in. And I am thinking and saying to myself, Good Lord, what the heck!

And now people were going nuts and, as a player, I was feeding into it—I could feel the excitement. The Lord hasn't made any words to describe how I felt. Between the adrenaline, the excitement from the crowd, entertaining the people, and having birdied every freaking hole, I was in the zone.

But still, at that time, my mind was not on the fact that I birdied every hole in the U.S. Open or that I was leading the U.S. Open. I didn't give either of those a second thought.

I was just there, and the ball was going where I wanted it to go.

Chapter 11

"The U.S. Open just takes so much discipline. You have got to be a great putter and just kind of let things roll off your back."
— Brooks Koepka

As we are walking to 7th tee, Bob Estes says to me, "Man, that has got to be some kind of record, birdieing the first 6 holes of a U.S. Open."

My response was, "Yeah...yeah, I guess so." I wasn't thinking about what I had just done. In fact, I wasn't thinking about anything. I had this little chip shot of a par 3 coming up. To me, that was more important than what may or may not have been a record.

Estes is as unassuming and well-mannered a guy as they come. Any mother would be proud to have him as a son.

There was no wind, so it was an easy shot. I had a little baby pitching wedge and hit it about 15 feet below the hole. Pars were good, so I was happy playing the percentages.

As I was standing on seven green, I glanced up at this big hill above us and there were thousands of people everywhere. I could see people walking down the eighth fairway backward to see us play. That made an impression on me, and you could just feel the charge in the air.

As fate would have it, I didn't hit a good putt. Then again, it didn't really bother me all that much because again, pars are very good at the U.S. Open.

On the eighth tee, I hit a good drive with a three wood and got it in the fairway. We had 181 to the hole and the pin was about 10 feet from the left edge and 20 feet onto the green. Not a good pin position for my little fade. It didn't fit my shot, so I took out a five iron and started it five yards left of the green—which was not a great choice—but I was hitting it so good it didn't matter. The idea of missing a shot never crossed my mind. The ball was still going exactly where I wanted it to. I just pulled the club, swung, and it was like the ball read my mind.

I hit a little three quarters five iron and from impact I knew it was perfect, just like the rest of them that day. It hit short of the hole and ran right by it, then stopped four feet above the hole. I dang near made it for a two. Marking that ball, 4 feet above the hole, meant there was never a question of me making the putt.

I was hoping to God to two putt. The greens were so fast, I felt like I should blow on the ball instead of putting it. There were people everywhere. I'd never had that many people watch me play golf before. Again, I didn't think about making the putt, I just touched it and the ball rolled down and missed the hole to the left and settled about four inches from the hole. There were groans from the gallery, but I was very happy to make par.

I had noticed how many spectators there were trying to see what was going on when I was on 5. By 8, the crowds were enormous and everywhere. The idea of complete silence before a golf shot is a joke and truly, the noise wasn't a big deal. These were my kind of people and I had become the underdog everyone was cheering for. I think I bogeyed 9, no 10, because I had a 30 on the front nine. I played the 9th perfectly with a good drive down the left side and a good iron into the green and then a good two putt for par.

I had just played the first nine holes at the U.S. Open—pain free. Every shot I had, I just looked where I wanted the ball to go, and every time it went where I wanted it to go. If I had played the rest of the tournament this way, well, I would have been the U.S. Open Champion and in the Masters.

The 10th hole was quite a way from the clubhouse. I teed off on 10 and my drive didn't fade. I was just in the rough. I remember this like it happened yesterday. The marker had a flag by my ball and when Weed and I got up there, he picked up his marker. We were standing close by getting our yardage but when we looked back down, we couldn't find our golf ball. So Weed and I had to look for my ball for 30 seconds—which seemed like an eternity. A lost ball after the marker finding it? Come on!

I didn't need a yardage, just my sand wedge to gouge it out 10 yards or so into the fairway. And Weed said, "Yeah, you're right, just get it out onto the fairway."

So, I did, and I still had 165 yards to the green. I knocked it on and two putted for an easy bogey—no problem—I was still playing well. But it was my first bogey—on number 10.

It was a tee ball bogey because I missed my target by two feet and had a one stroke penalty for hitting in the rough.

Over to the 11th, I had a cute par 4 that was a dogleg from left to right that suited my eye perfectly. This was my kind of shot—a perfect tee shot. I got up there and had a blind second into the narrow green. I hit a cut 9-iron that was good, but when I reached my ball, it was about 15 feet above the hole—which is not a good thing at Pebble in the U.S. Open. So, it wasn't a putt I could really run at, obviously, so I hit a little putt down 3 feet from the hole and made it for par.

Things were fine. I felt great. I was still on the leaderboard and the entire crowd was cheering for me. Bubba—I had never been called Bubba before, but it seemed to fit, and I enjoyed it. I was the underdog, the people's choice, and the guy who no one had heard of, and I was leading the U.S. Open.

Number 12 was a par 3. The pin was front right, which is a little bitty area—a nook in the green. I hit a good 7-wood down there on the front right fringe. I was already comfortable with the 7-wood no different than every other club in my bag. It was kind of ridiculous. I two putt for par.

The 13th was a simple hole, but it had rough and the green had a huge slope from back to front.

From the 13th through the 17th hole, I wasn't sure where I made a bogey. I was in total control, and everything felt easy. The most important thing was I was in control of my mind and my emotions. If someone had taken my blood pressure at that moment, it would have been low. And the reason was like I said, being broke sucks. Being broke overpowered any excitement or euphoria of playing in the U.S. Open.

It was more that the depression of being broke far outweighed the exhilaration of being in the U.S. Open. I was used to being broke and played well because of it.

Chapter 12

"I gather most people don't remember that when the U.S. Open first went to Pebble Beach in 1972, a big deal was made of the Open going to a public course for the first time." — Dan Jenkins

On the 18th, I drove it in the fairway and then laid up with my 2nd shot, with a 4 iron, because the farther you hit the 2nd shot, the narrower it got. The weather was still nice—no wind, no rain. That tee shot was scary because on that hole to play a cut, you have to play it out over the ocean a little bit. I was standing on the 18th tee with people behind and all around me. I remembered the practice round when starting the ball left was easy and the ocean was beautiful. But in the tournament, it wasn't as easy, and the ocean was disastrous. You are thinking, This ball needs to cut but if I cut it too much then I am out of bounds.

So, I set up and hit it perfectly down by the tree on the right side and then hit a good lay up, so I had a cut 9 iron into a front right pin location. I hit it about 15 to 20 feet from the hole and then cozied it down there for a tap-in par. It had been a magical day. People were yelling and screaming and chanting my name. They had been drinking all day. It was like a scene out of Tin Cup or Happy Gilmore. Those were movies. Mine was real life.

At about 11, I became aware of the cameras and the legend Chris Berman. The U.S. Open was big, Chris Berman was bigger. He had been sitting off the fairway by himself, watching me and wondering who I was and what the heck was going on. I had Chris Berman watching me and Weed carrying my bag; I couldn't have dreamed this. I had known that I was a crowd favorite from after the first six holes. After the first six holes, I sensed this was my U.S. Open, no one else's. I was the guy at that moment in time at the U.S. Open and I could feel it after putting out on the last hole. Then, after signing my scorecard, I thought I would get a bite to eat and then hit a few putts. My girlfriend, Tammy, was with me, along with my caddy, Weed.

I was totally wrong. A USGA official came up to me and said, "I need to take you to the media tent."

I said, "ok" but I was thinking, Holy cow, I have never done this before.

So, he loaded us up on this golf cart and drove us to the media tent. When we got there, he asked me if I wanted something to drink so I said, "Yeah, a water would be fine." We entered this large circus tent and he told us to wait, so we waited.

There must have been 300 to 400 people from the media in the tent that day and they had a table with some lights shining on it on a stage. When it was my turn to be interviewed, I had to sit at the table behind a mic and answer questions from the media.

First, they went over my round and then the questions began to get more personal. They didn't know anything about me. I had been on tour before with a little success, but not enough to become a household name.

They asked me where I had been playing and I told them I'd been in mini tour tournaments in places they had never heard of and so on. They asked if I had been playing well and I said yes and that I had been on tour before, etc. They asked me if I felt any pressure from playing the U.S. Open, I told them playing in the U.S. Open was easy. Real pressure is trying to make a six-footer, knowing you had to make it to pay your next truck payment.

And then, I will never forget, someone asked me what winning the U.S. Open would mean to me and I said it would mean GMAC would quit calling me about when I was going to send them my next truck payment.

They loved it. They thought I was kidding but I was dead serious. I had sat in the gin room at Oak Tree too many times when Nate had paged me saying, "Andy, you have a call on line 2." It was GMAC asking me where their money was. Actually, winning the U.S. Open was a means to an end. I needed the money and I wanted to play in the Masters. If I won, the U.S. Open trophy would just sit on my mantel and do nothing. It certainly wouldn't be paying my bills.

I was just telling the truth—I didn't know any other way but to be honest. I wasn't trying to win sympathy or anything else. It was what it was, and they asked, so I answered. It hadn't sunk in what I had done that day. I was emotional because of the day I had just had. I had been blessed to have a day in golf that no one else had ever experienced. I didn't fully understand that this day would change the rest of my life. Nor did I understand the true purpose of this day for a full 29 years. Still, something I will always remember was Willie telling me to be sure to tell them how much we talked about getting a good start and give me a chance to get on TV. It was a task we talked about often because, not to beat a dead horse or anything, but I needed the money.

And I did. Willie and I had fun that week at Pebble Beach, a week we will both take to our graves.

Chapter 13

"The whole secret to mastering the game of golf—and this applies to the beginner as well as the pro—is to cultivate a mental approach to the game that will enable you to shrug off the bad days, keep patient and know in your heart that sooner or later you will be back on top." — Arnold Palmer

I couldn't have asked for a better first day. Tammy and I headed back to the house, the tiny little house we were renting with Willie for the week, and Willie was sitting on the couch, watching television, and smiling. He started laughing as I walked through the door.

I looked at him and the first thing I asked was, "Was I on TV?"

Willie looked at me and said, "On TV? Hell, you were TV!"

"Really?" I asked.

And he said, "Are you kidding, hell yes! You were all over it."

Willie had shot par or a couple under and that is always good at the U.S. Open. Six pars are equal to a birdie in the Open, so he'd played really well.

Both of us were pumped because we were both playing really well. Here we were, staying in a tiny cheap rental and we were both playing really well in the U.S. Open. Could it be better? I knew I had made some money—which was my number one goal—by getting on television. In my mind, I had already had one win at the U.S. Open. Millions of people were watching me on TV—that is a big deal. It was as if a giant weight had been taken off my shoulders, and, in reality, it had. I was so concerned about bringing in some cash, I wasn't enjoying the Open like I could have been.

Looking back, perhaps having something else on my mind besides my golf game wasn't a bad thing. It probably kept me from overthinking. Not that I played poorly the rest of the tournament, because you have to be good to get into the tournament, but having a distraction probably helped. Friday, I no longer had that distraction.

It had been a long day and I was tired. We were all tired and wanted to rest. This was, after all, the biggest tournament of our lives. We made some dinner and relaxed. Grabbing a bite to eat in Pebble isn't a quick one-and-done, especially when there were thousands upon thousands of tourists in town for the tournament. The wait times could be hours. It's a major ordeal and none of us were up for that.

I had talked to my parents Thursday night because of how well I played, Let's face it, it's not often a normal everyday person is on television. It was a huge deal for me and our family because I was on TV. They were very excited—their son was in the mix at the U.S. Open. Growing up at Briarwood in Tyler, Texas, to playing at Pebble in the U.S. Open is a heck of a journey. I was a bit of a hometown hero at that point and my parents were enjoying the tournament more than I was.

My mom asked about my hair because I had let it grow long and had gotten a perm before the tournament, which was a different look for me. Of course, she would notice my hair. That is how moms are, right?

That first day was emotionally draining but I slept well that night. We had that house two blocks from the water and the house had no air conditioning, so we slept with the windows open. Hearing the waves all night long lulled me to sleep so I slept soundly. It was nice and cool, and anytime I woke up, I would hear the waves and drift back off to sleep. I was playing in the U.S. Open and I could hear the water meeting the shoreline. This was the life I'd always wanted. It felt good.

The entire time I was at the tournament, even on the charter flight, I felt like I had a secret that no one else had. And looking back, I did.

A big part of it was Verplank and him telling me to hit the ball where I was looking. Verplank is a world class golfer and getting that advice from him really impacted my game. I'll always be thankful.

Friday morning, I felt great. I arrived at my locker to find the shirts Fred Couples left for me along with the note that read, "These are for you. I hope they help out. Good Luck." That was a really good start to day two.

My tee time on Friday was 2:20 pm, so I had a lot of time that morning. For a professional golfer, the time off the course is as important or maybe even more important than the time on the course. It is so important to keep your mind organized off the course, just like you try to do on the course. And the great players know how to do that. They would set small attainable goals, like, I won't make nothing worse than pars all day as a daily goal. Well, if a golfer hit that goal enough times in a day, they would win the tournament. It was one mental way to keep you from getting ahead of yourself.

You also have to keep your mind off of golf when you're not on the course. The tendency of many inexperienced players is to let their mind wonder about what might be.

At the end of the first day, I was the underdog story of the U.S. Open and the buzz—all the attention—was something I had never experienced and keeping my mind from racing was tough. I knew I had to relax and not allow myself to think about being near the lead of the U.S. Open, but it was an entirely new experience, and I wasn't very good at ignoring my feelings or the notoriety.

I was born in 1961 so I was 31 years old when I played at the U.S. Open. I had experienced everything by then—tournaments, winning, losing, living—everything except playing well in the U.S. Open.

Being unfamiliar with the crowds, the attention causes problems with your brain, which is your computer, and that can lead to problems with the technical side—the ball striking. When I woke up on Friday, it was overcast and foggy, just a typical day at Pebble since it is so close to the ocean. Being from Oklahoma where we can see temperatures in the 90s or even the 100s, the temperature was cool.

I was one of a handful of players who didn't wear a sweater. I didn't need one. For me, Friday was the perfect golf day.

It was the second day of the U.S. Open and there were only a few people watching us warmup because the practice area is quite a way from the course. So far so good. When I arrived at the course, I got off to a good start, a steady start. When I do that, the nerves start to settle and I'm able to focus. I bogeyed one of the first holes, then eagled the sixth hole. The noise was really loud the second day.

There was just an aura about the tournament, something that is hard to explain. I like to say that the strongest things in the world are the things you know are there, but you can't see.

With a 2:20 pm tee time, Friday afternoon at the U.S. Open, we had a large crowd that was jacked up—in fact, it was a bit of a spectacle. I had a lot of fans following me Friday, and it was the people who enjoyed the person they considered the underdog versus the big names. From the articles already published, people knew about my life and my financial troubles. I was the one they could relate to because for many of them, they were where I was or had experienced what I was experiencing sometime in their past. Most of the spectators at the Open had no idea what it was like to play a game of golf and win a million bucks. But most knew what it was like to miss a truck payment. I was their guy.

Let's face it, that was my tournament. I was the John Daly character in it and though Tom Kite won it and his name is on the trophy, that 1992 U.S. Open was my tournament. And, comparatively speaking, no one made more money than me. It was just a great week.

Chapter 14

"If I had only one more round to play, I would choose to play it at Pebble Beach. I've loved this course from the first time I saw it. It's possibly the best in the world."
— Jack Nicklaus

In a practice round that week, we played through Jack Nicklaus and David Duval, and I knew them both. I was playing with Willie, and we may have signed up to play with them because you could do that: just write your name down to play with whoever is in that time slot.

But when we got there, they had already teed off. Sometimes the well-known golfers do that because they already know who they want to play with. I think that's what they did that day because they were hitting a lot of balls and taking a lot of putts.

They had their reasons. We were all there to do one thing, play our best golf. Willie and I didn't let it bother us. We were there to win too. Playing with Jack and David would have been great, but it wasn't our end goal.

In my practice rounds, I would figure out where the USGA was going to put the pins and practice putts and chips to those areas. The practicing short game around the green and on the greens were much more important than anything else.

By the way, it was Jack who said later in the week, "Andy Dillard is not entirely unknown." Jack said I had played on the tour and played well. And that is something I still cherish—a compliment from the greatest golfer of all time.

I was not uncomfortable that second day and I was smart enough to avoid reading the papers. I know Jim Murray of the Los Angeles Times wrote a piece that was good—very clever. Several years earlier, Willie and I had called him to complain about him calling us less than talented at the LA Open at Riviera. But Murray now had a piece telling the world I had done something never done by Nicklaus, Hogan, or even Bobby Jones, and that the golf gods might excuse a legend for making 6 birdies in a row to start the U.S. Open, but not an Andy Dillard. He said the golf gods would exact their revenge and was even pleasantly surprised that I had not shot a 45 on the back nine or something similar to that.

The second day went well, though not as spectacular as day one. I was making a lot of pars, which are great at the U.S. Open. I know that sounds redundant but it's true and it was a mantra for me that week and I think it helped. Nothing more than a bogey. I told myself that over and over again. I did make an eagle on the sixth hole that helped my score that second day and then there was one very cool shot that I will never forget.

I was pretty dead on the par 5 14th that second day, laying three left of the green with an impossible flop shot that I just wanted to make sure I hit hard enough for a chance for a par and no more than a bogey; in fact, I would have taken bogey and been happy. I later heard a lot of guys were sitting around the clubhouse in the locker room watching on TV and everyone said, "No way Andy gets it up and down." Well, I hit it just perfectly and it one hopped into the hole for a birdie. All the people watching us had been drinking all day and the crowd was going nuts.

I proceeded through the next three holes and got to the 18th that second day knowing a birdie would give me a 70 and still close to the lead as Gil Morgan, my neighbor, so to speak, was out in front of the pack at that point.

The last hole of the second day, it was getting late, and a lot of people were still following us. I remember seeing the scoreboard and thinking, Holy cow, if I birdie the last hole, I am playing in the final group on Saturday.

That was a big deal to me. And so, I hit a good wedge about 10 feet below the hole. I had a left to right uphill putt, and I knew I was going to make it. So, there I was, to be playing in the final group the next day at the U.S. Open.

You might say, it was at that time I thought to myself, I am in the last group tomorrow in the U.S. Open. Ten or so days before I was playing in a mini tour event in Houston with people telling me to speed up because I was in the last group there and we were holding them up. Talk about no respect, but that was the mini tour in those days.

But now I am in the last group at Pebble Beach, just completed the first 36 holes, and I knew I had that check coming as well. Life was good and about to get better.

Being the people's choice meant more than a crowd of fans. The press also wanted to know who I was. I'd not made the papers, other than locally, for any golf event in quite some time. What I'd learned later was, a reporter by the name of Michael Madden for the Baltimore Sun happened to be watching me along the fairway trying to figure out where I had been and where I had come from.

This is from an article in the Sun from June 19, 1992" ""I wonder what he's been doing the last few years,' I (Michael Madden) said. The golf junkie only shrugged his shoulders.'

""He's been playing the Texas Tour and mostly staying at home,' said a woman to our right. We looked to our right. There was a blonde lady, youthful and pretty, looking a bit proud, too. 'That's what he's been doing.'"

Michael realized he had an Andy insider and continued to pepper her with questions as they walked and Tammy talked. He'd struck gold!

Speaking of the press, Chris (Boomer) Berman had been watching me play the first two days. I had noticed him off by himself halfway through the first day. He would sit in his golf cart off to the side. Chris Berman was, and still is, an absolute legend for ESPN Sports. He took the job of news anchor with ESPN back in '79 when most people thought a television channel entirely dedicated to sports was a crazy idea. He thought otherwise and was the face of ESPN from then forward.

I finished up and was in second place on the scoreboards. I went to hand in my score card at the trailer and afterward, there, bigger than life, was Chris Berman. The man is, what 6'5", 6'6", and must have weighed 300 pounds. He had just as big a presence on ESPN. He approached me and introduced himself, "Hi, I'm Chris Berman."

Now imagine with me if someone you'd watched on television for years approached you and introduced himself, as though you might not know who this person was.

I said, "I know who you are. I watch you on TV all the time."

He started laughing and asked if he could interview me. What? Of course, he could interview me. The guys running around in golf carts wanted me to head to the media tent to be interviewed. I told them Chris was first. He asked me questions about me and my golf game, but I will always remember the advice he gave me: "Don't be nervous and keep playing the way you're playing."

I told him, "I wasn't nervous. If I had been nervous, I wouldn't have been playing the way I was."

We chatted for a while, and I enjoyed every minute of it.

The end of day two had me in second place. The top 16 with a tie would go to the Masters. My dream had been to play in the Masters. I was on my way.

Chapter 15

*"You are going to hit some good shots and not
get rewarded, but that's just U.S. Open golf.
It's tough; it's hard."* — Peter Uihlein

Saturday, since I was in the last group of the day, I
had a lot of time to just do nothing. Nothing
means too much time to think, to wonder, to
speculate on what might or might not happen. I'd
been playing professional golf for eight years. In
those eight years, I'd stood on the practice green
more times than I can count. Not once, in all those
years, did I ever stand alone on the practice green
and never once did the crowd surrounding the
practice green have all their attention on me. Along
with the U.S. Open, this was another first for me.
Saturday afternoon, after warming up putting for
fifteen minutes, Weed, Tammy, and I made our
way to the first hole. I had to make my way

through the crowd to get to the tee box. When I did get through, there were people 15 to 20 deep around the tee box, down the left side of the fairway, around the green, then down the entire other side of the fairway. I had never had that many people watch me play and knowing they were all there to see me, that every single person was watching me, well, it was a little unusual. Thursday, nearly no one was watching, and by the end of Friday, the crowd had grown, but what I experienced Saturday morning was unlike anything I'd been around and probably will never again. It was truly a once-in-a-lifetime experience.

Being last to tee off, which also meant I was in the last group of the day at the Open, came with its own set of issues. I wasn't exactly nervous, but I wasn't unaware of my surroundings either. It was a scene I knew wasn't normal. There were a lot of fans watching me. I knew a lot of responsibility came with that—responsibility to the crowd, to the game, and mostly, to myself. I couldn't let that get to me, not if I wanted to win. But I'd never been in this place before. I had led hundreds of golf tournaments in my life but never in the U.S. Open. I was having trouble convincing myself this was just another 18 holes of golf. I didn't know how to mentally separate what was happening around me and what I needed to focus on. Much has changed in the world, and we now have ways to calm our minds and spirits to block out the noise and focus. In '92, we didn't have a name for it, but I still tried to play tricks with my mind and tell myself this wasn't a big deal, when in reality it was the biggest stage I'd ever been on—it was the U.S. Open. Mostly, I liked to have fun, goof off, talk smack, and win some money. I enjoyed my life and I loved golf.

I turned to Weed and asked, "Can you believe this?"

He said, "What's that, man?"

I said, "Here I am in second place in the U.S. Open and all these people are here watching and two weeks ago, I was playing in Houston on a mini tour event and people behind us were yelling at us to hurry up and get out of the way. This is crazy."

Was I nervous? No. But, we're splitting hairs here because I did have some anxiety. I wasn't as laid back as I'd been on days one and two. I didn't know it until the tee shot on the second hole.

I was paired with a friend of mine, Gil Morgan, who was in the lead, and I was in second at the start of the day. Gil's from Edmond, Oklahoma, and a friend so it was a really good pairing.

The USGA makes sure the third and fourth rounds of the U.S. Open are nothing like they were the first two days. To explain this, the pin placements are a little more difficult on Saturday and Sunday. Let's face it, the fans want to see birdies, but the USGA wants to see pars. The USGA wants to see what we're made of. Everything is more difficult, as it should be. This is the U.S. Open.

On the second hole, which is an easy par five, the first two days I birdied. Suddenly, my ball didn't drop to the right. My tee shot didn't fade, instead it went straight into the left rough. I ended up with a bogie on hole two—a hole I should have made an easy birdie on.

The weather was fantastic, and I was feeling good. Gil was doing great. By the sixth hole he was 10 under—the first person in U.S. Open history to hit double digits under par. I bogeyed hole six, an easy par five I birdied on the first two days. My tee shots kept going straight instead of dropping to the right and ending up in the fairway. I was in a foot of rough. At the end of the day, each fairway you miss is a penalty shot. You could just add one to your scorecard.

I wasn't playing terrible; I just wasn't playing from the fairway. I was getting frustrated because I wasn't miss hitting in a big way; I was just barely missing the shots by a few feet, but the penalties were still severe. None of which did much to help settle my nerves. I hadn't been in that situation enough times on that big of a stage to know to step back and adjust. I kept going with what I knew. Saturday, I bogeyed the golf course to death.

On hole 13, I was waiting on Gil to tee off because whoever made the lowest score on the hole before tees off first. I knew I was going backward instead of forward—that I was losing my spots and I kept dropping farther down the leaderboard. I was leaning on my driver and Gil looked over and I asked him if he was going to hit. He responded, "You're up." My thought was, I know I've been making a bunch of bogies, but if I'm up, you must have had a wreck.

Here I was, not focused. I got a little worried that I might be affecting his game negatively. Normally, when you're paired up, you feed off one another and you play similar to the other. If one is doing good, then the other will get motivated by their energy and play well too. I felt bad that I wasn't playing the way I had the previous two days.

I told him, "Hey, this isn't hard. Let's finish this thing. Let's make the best of it." He agreed and he finished the day strong. I wasn't as fortunate as he was, and I ended up with a 79 on day three. Day one and two, I shot 68 and 70, respectively.

Suddenly, I'm no longer the crowd favorite. They forget about you fast and move to the next great thing. The feeling was immediate and very noticeable. My U.S. Open took a turn for the worse and I wasn't entirely sure of why it changed but I needed to get my game back on track. It was disappointing as heck. I wasn't thinking about the Masters—which had been my lifelong dream—at least not yet. I wasn't a strong enough player—a strong enough person—to take a step back and say time to regroup, time to rethink this and change perspective. The importance of the U.S. Open had finally caught up to me. Golf is a mental game; everything starts with your mind. I've learned that now. Then, it was so overwhelming. Between how I was playing, the media, and all the fans, I just kept going the same direction and when I look back, I realize I wasn't in a bad place at that point. I could have still pulled off winning the U.S. Open and making it into the Masters if I had I taken the time to pause and reflect. Our minds are powerful. We can change so much by changing our thinking. I just didn't know it then. I was in a place I was unfamiliar with, and it just got the best of me.

At the end of Saturday, I went to the media tent and, basically, they wanted to know what happened. I told them the same.

Saturday was the longest day of my life. I knew I was bleeding to death, and I just didn't know how to stop it.

Chapter 16

"It goes without saying that my biggest disappointment was never winning the U.S. Open. I'm reminded of it all the time. It hurts when people remember you for the things you didn't do, rather than for the things you did do." — Sam Snead

Sunday morning, I woke up to 30-mile per hour winds coming in off the Pacific. I knew this day was going to be brutal. The USGA, Pebble Beach, and Mother Nature were in agreement to make this day the toughest day ever played in the U.S. Open to date. Nobody knew what a good score would be on Sunday.

I took some time to mentally prepare. I was still in this. I knew I could win, I just had to make sure the day before was over.

Birdies were almost non-existent, and pars were very difficult to make. It was nothing more than a day of survival. The first three days on the seventh hole—a short par three—I used a pitching wedge and barely tapped it. Sunday, the wind was coming off the ocean from right to left. I started with a four iron on the right side of the green and I tried to cut it, which means curve it back toward the right so I could hold it right there. The wind was so strong, my ball still ended up left of the green. It was absolutely crazy conditions.

No one was making birdies on Sunday, but I was making a lot of pars. The average score was 82 for Sunday, so Pebble Beach and Mother Nature were kicking everyone's butt. I couldn't make enough birdies to win, but I was playing great. I never gave the Masters a thought, not once that day. I was wanting to play as well as I could and finish strong.

Number 17 is the famous par three and it goes right back toward the ocean. We were dead into the wind waiting on the group in front of us to finish. Weed and I were standing there and Bambi, Willie's caddie, walks up to me and says, "Do you want to know where you stand at getting in the Masters?"

I really thought I was out of it, that I had no chance of making the Masters, so I was really surprised I even had a chance. I said, "Yes!"

He says, "Par, par, you're in."

What? All of a sudden, my lifelong dream to play in the Masters was still on the table. I thought that lifelong dream was gone, but not so. I had to make two pars. I knew 18 was a par five and if I could make par on 17, I was going to get in the Masters.

Weed asked me what I thought. The wind was still blowing 30 miles an hour, and the hole was 236 yards dead into the wind.

I told him I wanted to take a driver out, started left into the ocean and a high soft cut driver, which is a very risky tough shot to pull off. Very few people are able to make that shot and very few have it. I knew I had that shot. I could pick a freckle off your butt with my driver from 240 yards to 270 yards that week. Even though my fades hadn't been fading, initially that is what I wanted to do. I asked Weed, "What do you think?"

He said, "Hey, we're just trying to make three on this hole."

I said, "Yes, you're right. What do you think we should do?"

He said, "Let's just hit the 3-wood in the front bunker. It's an easy bunker shot and let's make three."

He asked what I thought, and I told him I thought he was right. And he was right. At the end of the day, no matter what my caddie told me, I was the one pulling the club and making the shot. I was responsible for making the final decision and the outcome was on me, no one else.

The problem was, I missed hit my 3-wood and it didn't get to the bunker, it came up short. My ball ended up in about a foot of rough and now, I had no chance of getting the ball close to the pin.

The best I could do was get it 20 feet past the hole, and if I did that, I'd have been happy.

I did just that. I hit a great putt and it went over the right lip and didn't go in, so I made bogey. Now, I I needed birdie on 18 to get in the Masters. Talk about pressure.

The 18th tee shot was very difficult because the wind was left to right and the hole doglegs to the left. I had to start my tee shot twenty yards left into the ocean to have a chance for my ball to be in the fairway, to which, as you can imagine, I had to be totally committed.

The shot didn't go where I wanted it to go, and I ended up in the rough. I had to lay up to a hundred and fifty yards from the green. The pin was cut barely short right over the bunker. The wind was 30 miles per hour left to right. I had to hit a perfect 7 iron to get barely over the bunker to get close to the hole for birdie. It ended up in the front bunker. I hit a great bunker shot three feet above the hole and made my putt for par, which was great because I didn't want to bogey on the last hole of the tournament. I didn't make the birdie and I thought my shot at making the Masters was done. My dream, the one thing I'd hoped for my entire life was over. In my mind, the great tournament I was having turned into a disaster. Depression hit me almost immediately.

As with anything in life, if we take the time to look at any situation, we can find the good. The pain and disappointment were too fresh for me to have an open mind about my tournament. A lot of good came from it. I made a bunch of money and would be able to make my truck payments for a while; I became a household name from being on television so much; Jack Nicklaus—an idol of mine in the golf world—had some really great things to say about me; I finished well in a major tournament; and I really had a great time. I didn't stop to think about how I opened the tournament, how unique it was to make birdies on the first six holes. I didn't come to see that accomplishment as the gift it was for quite some time afterward. I just figured my chance at the Masters was done.

Saturday's round left me in about 24th or 25th place, so there were still groups coming up behind us to finish out the tournament. Sunday, I shot 77, which was a great score considering the average was 82. Saturday was the day I lost the U.S. Open and was the day—I would learn later—that changed my life forever. Par was 70 and I shot 79.

To finish out the day, I had a few friends and an agent tell me one of the corporate tents wanted me to watch the rest of the tournament in their tent and if I did, they'd pay me $400 to have something to eat and a beer with the patrons in the corporate tent. I was like, well, why not, I could use the money. I could hang out and relax and enjoy the rest of the afternoon. Corporations pay to have tents at the Open. That's where they entertain their clients.

The open was over for me. I grabbed a cold beer, and we were watching the end of the tournament on television. It dawned on me that while I couldn't win the U.S. Open, there were four or so guys who were just ahead of me in score that if any of them bogeyed, I'd be in the Masters.

I allowed myself to hope. I forgot all about sportsmanship and began hoping not one of them but all of them would make bogies. Two of the four chipped in for birdies. I couldn't believe it and it was highly doubtful they would be able to make those shots again in their lifetimes. It came down to the last guy, Gil Morgan, who I had played with on Saturday. He was on the 18th hole needing an 8-foot putt for par. Whether he made or missed this putt, it wouldn't make any difference where he finished in the tournament. He was still going to make the same amount of money. Everything was the same for him. But, if he missed it, I got in the Masters.

Gil was waiting to putt, and I was getting excited. I still had a chance. I told Weed and Tammy, and whoever else happened to be sitting at our table, "I'm going to go tell Gil to miss the putt." I actually started to go tell him.

When he reads this—if he reads it—it will be the first he's heard this story because I've never told him this. I started to go ask him to miss it, but I didn't make it in time. He made the putt and that was my last chance to get into the Masters. If I had made it in time, Gil was the type of guy who would have probably missed the putt. He's that nice of a guy. Not everyone is like that, but Gil is.

At the end of the day, Tammy and I went out for a nice dinner, a little celebration. We'd been eating McDonald's as much as we could all week just to keep from spending too much, but one nice dinner to end the week seemed right. We were seated and people began coming over to our table congratulating me on the tournament, patting my back, and asking for my autograph. When we'd finished eating, our bill was $50 or $60 bucks and the waitress told us she'd had a lot of diners asking to pay our bill, but—she pointed toward a table— he was the one who bought our dinner.

As we left, we stopped by his table and thanked him. He told us how interesting I'd made the tournament and he really enjoyed watching me play. It felt good and it was humbling when I realized how many people in the restaurant recognized me from the tournament. For a short while, I was well known in the world of golf.

I didn't win the Open. I didn't make it into the Masters. But I did really well in the top tournament in the world and that was something to celebrate—if only I'd looked at it that way. I'd finished 17th in the tournament. First through 16th qualified for the Masters. All the good—being the 17th best player in the world, making birdies on the first six holes of the U.S. Open, doing something no one had ever done—and hasn't done since—took a back seat to my disappointment in not living my dream of being in the Masters.

Leaderboard, U.S. Open 1992

DILLARD Cont. From Page 1, Sec. 3

sticking a knife in my hand. There's nothing I can do to fix it. I just have to find something else to do that day. It could have picked a better time to happen."

Although his hand kept him from proving it, Dillard says he is sure he would have earned an exemption at Q-school and given the PGA Tour another shot for the first time since 1988.

"What's hard is, I'm playing the best golf of my life, and I have nothing to show for it," he said. "There's no comparison to how much better a player I am today than I was on Tour."

Dillard nearly had a chance to try to repeat his 1992 performance in last year's final round at Pebble Beach. His 77 gave him a finish of 8-over, good enough to win $18,000, but a 76 would have qualified him for this year's Open.

He holds no bitter feelings at all about his second-half total of 156 after a first-half 138. It was just part of the education process, he said.

"You hear about people being in the zone," he said. "I was in the zone. I stood on the first tee in the third round in the leader group, with people standing around 12-deep. I couldn't believe all these people were watching me play golf. I looked at my caddy and started laughing. But I was never nervous on one shot the whole tournament.

"What happened wasn't bad. I was lucky to be in the situation I was in. You've got to take the attitude that, even though it wasn't just another golf tournament, it really was just a golf tournament. It was a great experience for me, something I'll never forget."

The Oklahoma State All-America says he misses playing with college teammates David Edwards and Willie Woods in this year's Open, especially since he thinks Baltusrol is more favorable to his game than the Pebble Beach Links.

"I feel like on most of the holes, you can run the ball right up on the green. It doesn't look like birdies are as much of a premium. I think I could play it well," he said.

His fondest memories of last year's Open include having a day named after him in Tyler ("I'll always have a special place in my heart for Tyler") and keeping the media in stitches with stories about dares — like attempting to swim across a lake at Edmond's Oak Tree Golf Club in 36 seconds before a mouthful of seaweed thwarted him — and his nicknames ("Bubba" and "Bib" will stick, he said).

Dillard is hesitant at first about predicting a winner halfway through the third round of the Springfield, N.J., tournament. "Right now, Lee Janzen is looking pretty strong. I kind of look for my friend David Edwards to make a move. Payne Stewart is playing solid, too. All of these guys are obviously playing well."

At the close of the conversation, though, Dillard picks SMU graduate Stewart, winner of the 1991 Open.

"To me, he looks like he's been there and knows what it's all about."

Dillard has, too. Perhaps next year, he'll have an opportunity to continue his education.

—AP Laser

ANDY DILLARD WAVES TO GALLERY DURING 1992 U.S. OPEN
Tyler Golfer Looking Forward To Becoming Regular On PGA Tour

Andy Dillard, U.S. Open 1992

Part 3 – The Turn

Chapter 17

*"The only time my prayers are never answered
is on the golf course."* — Billy Graham

I wasn't ready to give up my dream. In fact, I fought tooth and nail to hang onto it. The year following the U.S. Open, I played some of the best golf I'd ever played. The better I played, the more the third day of the Open haunted me. Every time I thought about it, I would get irritated. I knew I could play better and my reasons for not playing well were plenty: the weather, the crowds, a bit of anxiety, my lack of experience on such a large platform…you name it, I used it as an excuse. Not once did I consider God's plan for my life. I was all about what I wanted. I had no intention of giving up.

That Saturday was the only day I didn't play really well the entire year. In fact, that day not only changed the direction of my golf game, but it also changed my entire life. It may be hard for some to understand just how powerful that one round of golf was, but that day changed everything. And at first, I didn't believe it changed my life for the better.

I spent the entire year preparing for the PGA Tour School, which is the qualifier to get back on the PGA tour. The qualifier is three stages. The first two are four rounds of golf and if a player makes it to the final round, he plays six rounds. 186 players are at the finals. The 50 lowest scores get their PGA tour card, which gives you a chance to play on the PGA tour the following year.

Because of the high level of my golf game, there was no doubt I would make it through the finals and qualify to get back on tour, which is where I belonged. Life was going along as planned, admittedly with a glitch, as I'd not accomplished what I'd wanted at the U.S. Open. But I could pick up and start again and get back to the Open the following year. The way I was playing, I was certain it would happen, and all would be right with my world.

As fate would have it, I was in Arizona for the finals of Tour School and I was warming up for the first round when I pulled a tendon in the top of my right hand, just above the index finger. I'd had this happen a few times before that year and I knew exactly what I'd done. I wouldn't be able to play in the finals—I wasn't able to hold a golf club. To start the opening round would have meant I kept another guy from trying to qualify—that's not who I was. I knew I'd never make it, not with my hand, so 30 minutes before my tee time, I withdrew. It was the right thing to do.

My year was shot. I didn't win the Open. I didn't get into the Masters. And now, I didn't qualify for the PGA Tour. Not qualifying for the PGA tour was what pushed me over the edge.

From 1993 until 2003, I continued to play golf, but I never again qualified to play in the PGA Tour. I had always enjoyed playing golf. Those ten years I continually compared the tournaments I was playing in—and how much money I was making— to the tournaments I wanted to be playing in and how much more money I'd be making if I'd been on the PGA Tour. I started grumbling and golf wasn't as fun as it had been. As each year went by, I knew I was getting closer to the end of my golf career. Tammy knew it was time too. The thought of not playing professional golf for a living severely depressed me.

Over the course of those ten years, I spent hundreds upon hundreds of hours sitting and staring at a picture of Saturday's leader board of the U.S. Open wondering what happened. I had a chair in my garage, the third garage which is my man cave of sorts, and I would stare at that picture. Just stare. Not watch television. Not listen to music. Just stare. I was obsessed with that day and how it happened and why it happened.

My wife, Tammy, was my biggest supporter. She made sure our bills were paid, our daughters were taken care of, the lawn was mowed, the house cleaned, and everything in between. She never once complained. She gave me the freedom to chase my dream while she worked a full-time job. I will always be grateful to her for all she has done. She too encouraged me to keep playing as long as I felt I had it in me.

I searched and studied, I was relentless in the how and the why. The sheer silence would have been frightening to anyone looking in without knowing why I was obsessed.

Nothing prepared me for life after playing professional golf. My childhood was spent dreaming about the Masters. My education was centered around golf. Everything I did for the first thirty years of my life involved golf. Now what?

I wasn't sure what I should do. I had lost my identity.

Chapter 18

"I wasn't born to be a golfer. I was born to be a child of God." — Webb Simpson

As a child, I'd gone to church with my parents every week. I'd been baptized. I knew about God and attended Sunday School every Sunday at the First Baptist Church in Tyler, Texas. But, like many children, I identified as a Christian because my parents were Christians.

At some point in a person's life, they have to make their faith their own.

From the 7th grade on, golf became the most important thing in my life. Golf became my god. I was self-centered—self-absorbed—probably one of the most selfish people to ever walk the earth. I realize all kids, and especially all teens, know everything. I was no different. Between 5th and

6th grade, I couldn't wait to be on my own to do what I wanted, how I wanted, when I wanted. The attitude didn't change all through college. I knew best and, while I had to follow Coach Holder's instructions, internally, I only wanted to do things my way and knew full well, as soon as I graduated, I'd be back in control. I'd do what I was told until I could do things the right way—my way. That proved to be absolutely disastrous.

Matthew 7:13-14 talks about there being two paths. One is wide and leads to destruction. This path is where those who are more concerned with themselves than anything else walk. This one is well travelled. The other path is narrow and fewer walk this path. The narrow path is for those who have God first in their lives and everything else is a distant second. I was traveling down the wide path—the one that leads to destruction.

My mother passed away in 1996. I was an only child, and my mother was the glue that held our family together. Nothing prepared me for her death. Two months later, I married the love of my life. Two big life events, one that broke my heart and one that helped mend my heart, added to the stress of my declining golf career. One year later, my first daughter was born. Suddenly I was in this place where I wasn't the most important person in my life. I had others I was responsible for, and at times I bucked at the change. Sin is attractive until it comes back to bite you in the butt. I had visible bite marks on my bottom. I realized I had to do things differently if I wanted everything life had for me and my family.

Each tournament I played in always took me one step closer to ending my career in golf. I no longer had fun. I no longer felt the joy I had always experienced on the course. After each tournament, I would be angry and bitter and wonder why I wasn't on the PGA tour. My god of golf had quit feeding my ego and had become something I always wanted more from. That is what sin does. You taste it and at first it tastes good. Then you get in deeper and deeper, and you're never satisfied. You always want more and by this time, you know the sin will end up killing you, but you can't stop, at least not on your own.

In 2001 I missed making the PGA Tour by one stroke. In 2002, I played in the buy.com tour, which is a level under the PGA Tour. It's basically the springboard to getting into the PGA Tour. I missed the cut in 8 or 9 tournaments by one stroke, which meant I made nothing. I was out of pocket for all my expenses—travel, hotels, food, pretty much everything. Life wasn't just about me any longer. I had a wife and daughter to care for. I couldn't go on the way I was going. I wasn't getting any younger, and while I was playing well, I knew

I wasn't playing where I wanted to, and my bank account was dwindling.

As I neared the ten-year mark following the U.S. Open, my wife and I decided to start attending church. We knew we would benefit as well as our daughters. We knew things had to change to have the relationship we both wanted. We also knew something had to change if we were going to be the parents we needed to be. Not only did we start attending church, but we knew in our hearts my days as a professional golfer were over.

When my wife and I had come to the conclusion it was time for me to retire from golf, I became depressed. I worked menial jobs like driving a dump truck, being a car salesman, and as a salesman in the oil and gas industry. I did what I had to do to help support our family. For the first time in years, I was making regular, consistent contributions to my family's income. My wife didn't have to wonder if we would have enough at the end of the week to see us through to the next. She'd been the consistent bread winner for so long, I cannot imagine the relief she felt knowing I had regular income. She had basically been a single parent while I was playing golf. While I missed golf tremendously, knowing I helped relieve the burden of providing for our family felt good. It was the right thing to do. It is what a father and a husband should do, and I was one step closer to who I was called to be.

In some ways, doing the job thing was easier than going to church. Not the physical act of going to church; that was easy. But building a relationship with Christ who thus far had only been a casual acquaintance. We had been on a wave from a distance basis and now, He was calling me to open up and give everything to Him. My tendency to be self-centered prevented me from giving in too easily. I wasn't ready to relinquish what I wanted. Yet, at the same time, I knew in my gut, I had to change. Everyone I loved was counting on me becoming who I was intended to be.

Chapter 19

"Golf is just an avenue for Jesus to use me to reach as many people as I can." — Bubba Watson

As a child, I had made a conscious decision to give my heart to Christ. This meant I gave Him control of my life to intervene as He saw fit. Christ won't make us do anything. But, when we ask Him to be the Lord of our lives, He takes that seriously.

He never left me. I didn't acknowledge him in all those years, but He was there the entire time. He was waiting for me to call on Him, to ask for guidance and to give Him the glory in what I was doing. He gave me the gift of golf, the talent I possessed. I never once gave Him credit. I never stopped and asked for His blessing. He watched as I stepped off the narrow path and started walking down the path of destruction. He patiently waited for me to realize what I was doing before stepping in and doing something drastic.

When I look back at that Saturday, and my level of play, nothing besides God stepping in and taking control makes sense. I didn't suddenly play horribly one day of the entire year. I didn't change how I was driving the ball. I didn't change how I was putting. I didn't change my approach. I didn't change my mindset. All those years of thinking and staring at the scoreboard never gave me all the answers I was looking for. It wasn't until I got down on my knees that I found the answers.

I knew what being committed meant. I lived golf both on and off the course. I refused to give up until doing so was the only choice I had. From childhood, I was singularly obsessed with golf. Now, I had to learn to chase after what mattered— the important things in life.

I can't help but think of Moses who travelled for 40 years through the desert with the promise land on the other end of that journey to be told he could only look at the promise land, never step foot into it.

God allowed Moses to know the people he led across the desert were entering the promise land. He allowed him to look upon that land flowing with milk and honey and that had to be enough for Moses. I believe Moses knew he'd blown it right after he'd struck out in anger. He was close to God, he had a relationship. We also know from Moses' past, he had anger issues and I believe the moment got the best of him.

Winning the U.S. Open and playing in the Masters was my promise land. I could see it. I could taste it. It was so close, the dream so real, to have it slip from my fingers was absolutely devastating. I can imagine me looking at the U.S. Open, knowing it was so close, within my grasp; to only have it taken away must have felt similar to how Moses felt. Then again, Moses had lived a life serving God and serving His people. He stepped out of line and God kept him from receiving the dream. My whole life I had lived for me, for my own glory. It was His grace and mercy that allowed me to taste my dream at all.

I had a lifetime of ignoring God and His will for my life. A lifetime of chasing my dreams. A lifetime of only being concerned about me. Even in my disobedience, God gave me a gift at the U.S. Open. I birdied the first six holes in the U.S. Open—something that had never been done before and hasn't been done since. That is what grace and mercy are. Grace is getting what you don't deserve—me getting those six in a row. Mercy is not getting what you do deserve.

I didn't deserve living a life and doing the things that many around the world only dream about. I didn't deserve the many blessings God in His mercy gave me anyway. I'm forever grateful for Christ and His willingness to shed His blood so I can spend eternity Him. He loved me that much—despite the many times I messed up. He's that good and He loves you just as much.

It doesn't matter what you've done or where you've been. His grace and mercy are big enough for all of us. If you're still breathing, you still have hope.

If you've been asking yourself, why is my life not going according to plan, perhaps you need to ask, what is God's plan for my life? Is this the road He wants me traveling down? Is this how I can bring Him glory and point others to eternal salvation?

I was headstrong. I'm not saying don't be determined. Absolutely dream big and go after your dreams. But first, be sure your dreams align with what God has for you. It doesn't pay to chase the wrong passions—those bring nothing but heartache and pain—both in our own lives and the lives of those we love. However, if you know what God has called you to do, and if you know He is leading you down that path, give it everything you have and never give up.

God is the author of our dreams. He expects us to give Him glory in return. Often, our dreams line up with our natural abilities. Too many times, we not only ignore the giver, but we also come to believe we deserve the gift or the natural ability we possess.

For the world, this is to be expected. For those of us who have a relationship with Christ, we are expected to give credit where credit is due.

He won't drop our dreams in our laps. He expects us to prepare. If we use God's Word as our example, we can expect to gather the seeds, prepare the ground, plant, harvest, then sell the crops. I'm not a farmer but I can see why this example was used again and again in the Bible.

The farmer had to work from sunup until sunset and he had to trust the Lord every step of the way. What if the wind blew the seeds? What if the rain came and the seeds were washed away? What if hail destroyed the plants? What if the price of crops dropped and the farmer didn't make the money he needed to survive? Every step of the way, the farmer had to trust God knows what is best for him and would work out everything for the farmer's good, according to God's plan.

This is exactly what God expects of every believer. He expects us to work like we're doing it all ourselves but trust like He's doing everything for us. It's a partnership between us and God. He's the one who gave us talents and dreams and created a plan for our lives before we ever took our first breath.

For me, I want the world to know I am finally giving God credit for the many gifts He's given me. I especially want to draw attention to what He did to save me from myself at the U.S. Open while also giving me something no one else has been given.

I'll forever be grateful He did what was necessary to turn me around and point me back to the path that is narrow and hard to find.

The wide path is easy to recognize. Most of the world is traveling down this path living life doing what they want when they want without regard for anyone around them or the One who gave them life to begin with. The narrow path is harder to recognize. You really have to be searching for it or you'll pass it by without a second glance.

Chances are, if you're reading this book, you've at least heard about Jesus, the One who died on a cross so you may have eternal life. If you haven't yet given your life to Christ, you need to do that today because tomorrow may never come. You may never have another chance.

If you have already given your life to Christ, but you aren't living a life that glorifies Him, then it's time to repent and get back on that narrow path. You don't want to stay on the path that leads to destruction. It may feel good for a moment, but what comes later brings nothing but heartache and pain.

My plan was to win the U.S. Open and play in the Masters. God's plan was to give me a U.S. Open record and write a book. His plans are perfect.

If you aren't sure how to ask Christ into your heart, then here is a prayer Billy Graham often used to lead people to Christ.

"Dear Lord Jesus, I know that I am a sinner, and I ask for Your forgiveness. I believe You died for my sins and rose from the dead. I turn from my sins and invite You to come into my heart and life. I want to trust and follow You as my Lord and Savior. In Your Name. Amen."

About the Author

Andy Dillard is a retired professional golfer who holds a record in the U.S. Open. He continues to enjoy time on the local golf course teaching others and talking smack with his golfing buddies. He is married to the love of his life, Tammy, and they have two daughters, Brittni and Holli. He lives in Edmond, Oklahoma, and is active in his church.

Andy enjoys connecting with audiences as he shares his experiences both on and off the golf course. His passion in life is sharing the gospel of Christ and seeing the transformation as a result. If you would like Andy to speak at your next event, contact him at www.andydillard.com.

You'll find Andy on Facebook, Twitter, Instagram, and LinkedIn.